D0918367

DATE DUE

NOV 7			
JAN 1 9 1984			

PEACEFUL FIGHTER
GANDHI

The Yin and the Yang, *an ancient Chinese figure, is symbolic for Century Books, since both negative and positive forces which the figure represents also shape the lives of famous world figures.*

According to folklore, the Yin and the Yang are present in all things, functioning together in perpetual interaction. This balance between opposing forces, and the influences, both good and bad, that have molded the course of history are accurately portrayed as background material in Century biographies.

PEACEFUL FIGHTER

GANDHI

*by Elizabeth
Rider Montgomery*

A CENTURY BOOK

GARRARD PUBLISHING COMPANY
CHAMPAIGN, ILLINOIS

For Lisa Phillips

For reading the manuscript of this book and checking the accuracy of its content, the author and publisher are grateful to:

Ashakant Nimbark, Ph.D.
Associate Professor of Sociology and Coordinator,
Social Science Division
Dowling College, Oakdale, New York

Cover art by Russell Hoover

Picture credits:

American Museum of Natural History: p. 101 (bottom)
Black Star: p. 101, top (Santosh Basak); 123, both (Bosshard)
Information Service of India: p. 18, 30
Radio Times Hulton Picture Library: p. 36, 122
United Press International: p. 137, 149, 152
Wide World: p. 57, 140, 143, 158, 163

Contents

1. Son of a Saint

Mohandas Gandhi stared in horror at the scorpion crawling across the floor toward his mother's brown foot. The little boy knew that the scorpion's sting was poisonous, and he screamed a warning.

"Ba! Look behind you! A scorpion! Kill it!" He would kill it himself, but he was afraid.

Putlibai Gandhi made no move to crush the deadly insect. Instead, she sat calmly while it climbed up on her bare heel.

"Our faith forbids the killing of God's creatures," she said. "You know that, Mohan. I will not harm any living thing."

Mohandas stood petrified with fright. The scorpion crawled around Putlibai's ankle. She bent over quietly and lifted it with her silk scarf. Then she carried it gently to the open window and shook it out into the courtyard.

"There," she said. "Now it can't harm me, and I have not harmed it. I have observed the ancient Hindu teaching of *ahimsa*, nonviolence."

It was the year 1876, and Mohandas Gandhi was seven years old. The town of Porbandar, where he lived, in the extreme western part of India, stood on the shore of the Arabian Sea. Mohandas' family lived in the Gandhi ancestral home, a large three-story house built around a big courtyard. As was the custom in India, his father, Karamchand Gandhi, known as Kaba, lived with his five brothers and their families. When Mohandas and his brothers, Laxmidas and Karsandas, married, they too would live in the same house, but their sister Raliat would go to live with her husband's people. Each family had its own suite in the Gandhi house.

Kaba Gandhi was the *dewan,* or prime minister, to the prince of Porbandar, a tiny kingdom of about 70,000 population. There were more than 500 of these native states in India, some large, some very small.

Mohandas was proud of his father, for he knew that the prince of Porbandar considered him a fearless, loyal dewan. Kaba was so honest he once resigned his position rather than tell an untruth. But he was also impatient and quick-tempered. Mohandas could not help being a bit afraid of him.

Mohandas never feared his mother, for she was kind and loving. Putlibai was Kaba's fourth wife, and much younger than he. Religion dominated her life. She spent hours in the temple, praying and offering sacrifices.

One day, when *Chaturmas*, the four-month rainy season, was approaching, Putlibai announced that she would eat only one meal a day until the monsoons ended.

"On days that I do not see the sun," she added, "I will eat nothing whatever."

Small as he was, Mohandas knew that if Ba made this vow, she would keep it at all costs. If Ba did not eat for weeks, she might fall ill, for she was rather frail. The children tried to get their mother to change her mind.

Putlibai could not be persuaded. "This fast will purify me," she insisted.

On the first day of Chaturmas, Mohandas went off reluctantly to the primary school where he had recently been enrolled. There, with other boys, he practiced writing the English alphabet in the dust of the schoolyard until the monsoon rains turned the dust to mud. When school was over he ran home quickly, anxious to find out if Ba had eaten anything. Besides, he was painfully shy and he feared that someone would speak to him if he loitered. The rain soaked his thin cotton clothes, but he knew they would dry fast in the hot climate.

Breathless, Mohandas entered the courtyard of the Gandhi home. His eleven-year-old sister Raliat stood in the doorway.

"Has she eaten, Raliatbehn?" Mohandas gasped. *Behn* means "sister." "Has Ba taken any food today?"

Raliat shook her head and her earrings jingled. "Not yet, Mohan. The sun has not appeared."

The downpour soon stopped and the sky cleared. Anxiously Mohandas and his sister scanned the sky. Their nine-year-old brother Karsandas joined them at their vigil, and all three waited impatiently for the sun to show its face.

Suddenly a gleam of sunlight pierced the clouds. With whoops of joy the children raced into the house to break the good news to Putlibai.

"Ba!" shrieked Mohandas at the top of his voice. "The sun is shining! Now you can eat!"

Putlibai came to meet them. "I must see the sun for myself," she said. She hurried out of the house, with her beautiful *sari* floating and shimmering around her. It was made of six yards of embroidered gossamer-like material, which was wound around her waist and fastened at one shoulder. A fold of the *sari* covered her head when she went outdoors.

The children followed their mother. "There!" cried Raliat, stretching her bracelet-ladened arm toward the sky. But a cloud had already covered the sun. Mohandas wanted to cry with disappointment.

Putlibai smiled cheerfully. "God does not want me to eat today," she said.

Mohandas could not understand why Ba undertook so many fasts; seldom did anyone else in the family go without food. He himself dearly loved to eat.

"Why do you fast, Ba?" he asked.

"I am trying to lead a saintly life, Mohan," she replied, "so I can be reborn into a higher caste when I die."

Mohandas had heard about transmigration of souls. Each person, Hindus believe, is born into a certain caste, or social position, and throughout life he must remain in it. Only by living a sinless life can a person be reborn, after death, into a higher caste, and then a higher one. If his life is evil, he will be reborn into a lower caste, or as an Untouchable. His soul might even enter a dog, or a cat, or a jackal.

There were four main castes in Hinduism, although each had many subdivisions. At the top was the Brahman caste, mainly priests and scholars. The second caste was the Kshatriya, mostly warriors and rulers. The Vaisya caste, to which the Gandhis belonged, was next. Vaisyas were chiefly merchants and farmers. Finally came the Shudras, or laborers and peasants.

Lowest of all in the social scale were the Outcastes, or Untouchables, who belonged to no caste whatever. They did the work that caste members refused to do, such as sweeping, scrubbing, washing clothes, cleaning toilets, and handling dead animals.

Nearly 50 million Untouchables of India were forced to live apart from other Indians, usually in dire poverty. They could not draw water from village wells, or even attend the temples, and their children were not allowed to go to school.

One day when Uka, the Untouchable household "sweeper," came to the Gandhi house to clean the toilets, Mohandas followed him around asking questions. When Putlibai found the little boy in the same room with Uka, she was horrified. She dragged him away, stripped off his clothes, and gave him a purifying bath.

"Why?" the little boy asked. "Why do I have to take an extra bath, Ba?"

"Because you have been defiled, Mohan," his mother replied, scrubbing his thin brown body vigorously. "You were in the same room with an Untouchable. You let his shadow fall on you, and it polluted you."

"How can a shadow pollute?" Mohandas asked. "Uka is kind."

"But he is Untouchable!" Putlibai cried. "You, a member of the Vaisya caste, must never let an Untouchable come near you!"

Mohandas still wondered why. Putlibai was totally illiterate. She could not explain Untouchability in a way that satisfied the alert, inquiring mind of little

Mohandas. Her three older children accepted what they were told without question, but not Mohandas.

Without understanding why, Mohandas knew that each caste had its own *dharma*, or duty. This was a strict set of rules for living. The rules covered not only details of worship but also the daily bath, daily laundering of one's robe, what to eat, whom to eat with, and so on. Hinduism was not only a religion, it was a way of life.

In the evenings Mohandas sometimes heard discussions of other religions. His father, as prime minister to the prince of Porbandar, met many different classes of people. Some of them came to his house. Although Kaba was a Hindu, he was tolerant of other religions.

Jain monks came often to the Gandhi house. Jains carried the principle of ahimsa, or nonviolence, to an extreme. They would not move outdoors after dark for fear of stepping on an insect. Putlibai admired the Jains and shared their belief in nonviolence.

Muslim Indians were frequent visitors at the Gandhi home, too. Their religion was called Islam. Like Hinduism, Islam was more than a religion, it was a way of life. Hindus and Muslims disagreed sharply about many things. Muslims believed in one God, whose prophet was Mohammed. They considered idols sinful. Hindus, on the other hand, believed that God took many forms, and their temples were full of idols. They thought that God returned to earth occasionally in an earthly body.

There were other points of conflict. Muslims abhored the Hindu practice of child marriage. Muslims killed cows and ate their flesh, while cows were sacred to Hindus and wandered at will in the streets and bazaars. Muslims believed that all men are born equal, and scorned the Hindu caste system. Intermarriage between the two faiths was strictly forbidden. Hindus were not even permitted to eat with Muslims.

Islam had more followers among Indians than any other religion except Hinduism.

There were other religious groups in India: Parsis, Sikhs, and Christians. Christians were not welcome in the Gandhi house, because Kaba believed they tried to force their religion on others.

Mohandas listened politely to conversations about religion but he didn't really enjoy them. Like most boys, he was more interested in playing than in thinking. He was too shy to make friends, but that didn't matter because he had plenty of playmates in the Gandhi joint-family household. He and his brothers and cousins played tennis, cricket, or *gilli danda*, a game played with a long stick and a sharp wooden peg.

The Gandhi boys loved to go down to the nearby Arabian Sea to romp and watch seagoing ships sail past. When it was time for supper, they would return home and wash their hands, faces, and feet. They brushed their teeth for fifteen minutes in the manner prescribed for their caste, using a toothbrush made of a twig. A Hindu would never use a toothbrush made from the hair of an animal because that would mean injury had been done to one of God's creatures. Then the boys rinsed their mouths the required number of times and they were ready for supper. At the sound of the gong they went out on the veranda where the rest of the family was assembling.

Everyone sat cross-legged on mats. Kaba or one of his brothers repeated aloud some verses of a religious poem such as the *Bhagavad Gita,* the *Song of God.* Servants passed food in beautiful silver or copper bowls and plates. Each person helped himself to the heavily spiced dishes with his left hand and ate with the fingers of his right hand. Meat was never served in the Gandhi household, since that would mean the slaughter of an animal. Vegetables, cereals, nuts, and fruits formed the basis of the family's diet.

As usual, Mohandas ate greedily. The rice and curry tasted especially delicious tonight, and so did the sweet wheat cakes. How he loved to eat! Only one thing detracted from his enjoyment of the generous meal: Ba wasn't there to enjoy it, too. Another foodless day had passed for his beloved mother.

2. Child Husband

Shortly before Mohandas' eighth birthday, his father left his post in Porbandar to become dewan in Rajkot, another tiny kingdom of India, 120 miles inland. Like the ruler of Porbandar, the prince of Rajkot ruled his people as he pleased, as long as what he did suited the British.

The English had come to India as traders about 250 years earlier. Gradually they had gained political power. For more than 100 years all of India, nearly 2,000,000 square miles, had been under British control. In the native states, British rule was indirect, through the Indian princes. In the rest of India, called British India, English control was direct and absolute. The British viceroy ruled as the agent of the English king. Englishmen made the laws and British governors and courts enforced them.

Kaba's duties and responsibilities in Rajkot were the same as they had been in Porbandar. The house to which the Gandhis moved was not as large as the ancestral home in Porbandar, and there was no seashore for the boys to play on. Otherwise, Mohandas' life was little changed.

When Mohandas was twelve, he entered the Alfred High School. As in all Indian schools, the lessons were in English.

During an examination that year, the English educational supervisor came to the school. As a spelling exercise, he gave Mohandas' class five English words to write. Mohandas wrote each word on his slate. He wasn't sure of the correct spelling of "kettle," but he did his best.

Suddenly he noticed that his Indian teacher stood in the aisle beside him. The man was prodding him with his foot, and nodding toward a neighboring student's slate. With deep shock Mohandas realized that his teacher wanted him to copy from his classmate's work!

Mohandas bent his head. He wouldn't dream of cheating, and he was horrified that his teacher expected him to.

When the test results were announced, Mohandas learned that every boy except himself had every word right. The teacher, who had wanted to make a good showing before the English supervisor, was furious.

"If it had not been for the stupidity of Mohandas K. Gandhi," he fumed, "my class would have had a perfect score!"

When Mohandas was eight, he moved with his family
to this house in Rajkot, where his father was *dewan*.

Mohandas had been taught all his life to be honest. He did not believe that honesty was stupid.

Mohandas and his brother Karsandas attended the same school. Their oldest brother, Laxmidas, had finished high school and obtained a position with a lawyer. He was now married, and so was Raliat, their sister. She had never gone to school, because girls were seldom given any education in India.

When Mohandas was thirteen he became aware of an atmosphere of excitement in the household. He and Karsandas were fitted for new clothes. Their mother and aunts spent hours sewing and cooking. Their father and uncles discussed money and budgets. Mohandas wondered what was going on.

One day Karsandas told him gleefully, "We are going to be married, Mohan! You, I, and one of our cousins will be married at the same time, in one ceremony."

Child marriages were very common in India at that time. Hindu parents usually arranged marriages for their children when they were little more than babies. The wedding took place later, sometimes when the girl was only five or six years old. Many Hindu girls were wives and even mothers by the time they reached their teens. They lived with their husbands about half the year, returning to their parents for long visits.

Hindu marriage customs required prolonged and expensive wedding preparation and celebration. Often a bridegroom's family went deeply into debt to provide a lavish wedding for a son. It was sensible, Mohandas knew, for his father and his uncle to plan a triple wedding for their youngest children.

The prospect of getting married pleased Mohandas. He would get to ride in a wedding procession, perhaps on an elephant. For days he would eat his fill of rich sweets and highly spiced foods. Afterward there would be a strange girl for a playmate. It all sounded like great fun.

Mohandas' prospective bride was Kasturbai Nakanji, whose father was a merchant in Porbandar and a friend of Kaba Gandhi. Like Mohandas, she was thirteen. They had never met.

For months the preparations continued. At last the time came for the child-bridegrooms to be taken to Porbandar for the multiple wedding. Mohandas enjoyed every minute of the five-day trip by bullock cart.

On the wedding day, the three little brides were carried in curtained litters to the Gandhi home, while musicians played and hundreds of wedding guests watched. In the courtyard, the girls stepped down, their faces covered with veils, because the boys should not see them until after they were married. As the brides walked into the big house, the guests threw flowers at them, and their pathway was soon covered with fragrant flowers.

Putlibai led the girls up to the ceremonial room, which was sweet with incense. Everyone else followed, and the wedding ceremony began. While the holy fire burned, Mohandas and Kasturbai sat side by side on their wedding dais or platform. Together they performed the *Saptapadi*, the seven steps that a Hindu bride and groom take together. At the same time they made the required vows of faithfulness and devotion. Then Mohandas lifted Kasturbai's veil. What a pretty face she had, with large, expressive black eyes! He knew he was going to like her.

Then Mohandas and Kasturbai put into each other's mouth the *Kansar*, the traditional wedding sweet. And so, at the age of thirteen the two children were married. A red dot was painted on Kasturbai's forehead, so that everyone would know she was a wife.

The wedding procession now paraded through Porbandar. It stretched through the streets for a quarter of a mile. The guests rode in horse-drawn carriages and bullock carts, on camels or in covered-chair litters. There were no elephants, as Mohandas had hoped, but brightly decorated horses pranced and paced. Mohandas rode one of them proudly, and Karsandas rode another. Drums beat loudly. The scent of jasmine and lilies perfumed the air.

Everybody in the town came out to watch. People called out congratulations to the bride and groom.

"May you have a hundred sons," was a common wish, "and no daughters!" Each time he heard this Mohandas smiled and nodded.

Back again at the Gandhi house, a great feast was served, with music, singing, dancing, and entertainment by magicians and jugglers. For several days the feasting and celebrating continued. When it ended, the young couple returned to Rajkot with Mohandas' parents.

Mohandas quickly became very fond of his pretty child bride, and he felt extremely self-important. He was a husband now, the head of his own family. A Hindu wife was supposed to obey her husband and gratify his slightest wish. It was going to be great fun, Mohandas thought, to give orders and see them carried out, after having had to obey parents and teachers all his life.

To Mohandas' disappointment, married life did not work out that way. Kasturbai, spirited and independent, had been spoiled by an indulgent father. She knew nothing of blind obedience.

"You are not to go out to play tomorrow," Mohandas would tell his wife at night. She spent her days in the women's part of the house, where no men were allowed. Mohandas could see her only in the evening.

"You must not even go to the temple without my permission," he said sternly.

"I'll go out to play if I feel like it," Kasturbai would retort indignantly. "And I certainly intend to go to the temple."

"You must do as I tell you!" Mohandas shouted. "I am your husband!"

"You are not my jailer! I will do as I please."

Sometimes a quarrel became so violent that the two children did not speak to each other for days.

After a few months, Kasturbai learned how to keep peace with her jealous boy-husband and still avoid submitting to his tyranny. When Mohandas told her not to go to a certain friend's house, she listened quietly, dutifully, without a word of protest. But the next day she did exactly as she pleased. Sometimes she went out of the house more than she really wanted to, just to demonstrate her independence. She kept her face covered, for no Indian wife should be seen by any man except her husband or her sons.

Mohandas raged and stormed, but Kasturbai only listened submissively, and he knew she would do the very same thing the next time. He was actually helpless against Kasturbai's passive resistance.

Kasturbai had not learned to read or write, and Mohandas decided he would teach her. However, she did not want to learn; none of her friends knew how, and she could see no use for reading and writing. She would much rather learn from Putlibai how to cook and sew. Besides, Mohandas was not a patient teacher. When she made mistakes he lost his temper and yelled at her. Then she refused to try at all.

Even though Mohandas and Karsandas were married, they did not have to go to work and support their wives. In the joint-family household, all members were supported from a common fund. The boys were expected to continue their education. Karsandas, however, soon dropped out of school.

Kaba urged Mohandas to keep on with his education. "When I retire as dewan to the prince of Rajkot, I want one of my sons to take my place. A good education will be of great help in getting the post."

So Mohandas continued his studies at the high school. In spite of his shyness, he turned to other boys for companionship, now that his brother no longer accompanied him. When he was about fifteen, Mohandas chose as his special friend Sheik Mehtab, a Muslim Indian boy who was older than he. Mehtab was big, strong, handsome, and a champion athlete. He could run faster and jump higher than any of the other boys. Mohandas, undersized and conscious of his large protruding ears and his total lack of good looks, admired the Muslim boy. He wished he could be like him.

Kaba tried to discourage friendship with a Muslim. "I have heard," he said, "that Mehtab is a wild sort of fellow. He will have a bad influence on you, Mohan."

"Oh, no, Father," Mohandas protested. "Mehtab will not influence me. I will reform him." Like many young people, Mohandas wanted to prove that he knew more than his parents.

A few days later Mehtab asked Mohandas if he had ever eaten meat.

"Certainly not!" Mohandas replied. "It is forbidden by my religion. I have never even seen any meat."

Mehtab laughed scornfully. "That's why you are so weak and skinny. All big, strong people eat meat. Look at the English. Consider how powerful they are. Why, only a few Englishmen control hundreds of millions of Indians! And the British, of course, eat meat daily."

Mohandas envied Englishmen. They were so self-confident. They demanded—and got—instant obedience from the Indians who worked under them.

In a way he admired the British, too. It could not be denied that they had greatly improved communication in India by building roads, railroads, and telegraph lines. They had also established schools, colleges, and newspapers. However, Mohandas resented the attitude of Englishmen toward India's history and culture. They seemed to think that Indians had nothing to be proud of, yet India's history went back many thousands of years. When England was only an island of savages, India had had a fine civilization. Now, of course, England led the world in education, science, and industry, and the British Empire reached around the globe.

"I wish," said Mohandas, "the English would let us rule ourselves."

"As long as Hindus refuse to eat meat," Mehtab said slyly, "Indians will never be strong enough for self-rule." As a Muslim, meat-eating was not a sin to Mehtab. He quoted a verse that Mohandas had heard before:

> *Behold the mighty Englishman,*
> *He rules the Indian small,*
> *Because being a meat-eater*
> *He is five cubits tall.*

To Mohandas, who was so small, it often seemed that Englishmen were, indeed, as the rhyme said, five cubits, or nearly eight feet, tall.

Day after day Mehtab continued to tempt Mohandas. "If you eat meat you will be brave like me," he said.

Mohandas had little courage. Many things frightened him—burglars, ghosts, and snakes. He was even afraid of the dark, and always insisted on a light in his bedroom at night. At last, hoping to gain strength and courage, Mohandas agreed to try meat.

The two boys met secretly one evening at an isolated spot on the river bank and shared a picnic supper of goat's meat and bakery bread. That night Mohandas had nightmares. In spite of this he tried another meal a few weeks later . . . and then another . . . and another. In time, he came to enjoy eating meat.

However, his conscience bothered him. He knew how shocked his parents would be if they discovered that he was breaking one of Hinduism's most rigid dietary laws and ignoring the prohibition against eating with a Muslim. Besides, every time he ate with Mehtab, he had to make some excuse when he got home for his lack of appetite.

Finally, Mohandas decided that he would eat no more meat in secret, nor would he hurt his parents by eating it openly. So the meat feasts ended.

The friendship with Mehtab ended, too. Mohandas decided that his father was right. He had made no progress whatever in reforming the Muslim boy, while Mehtab had had a bad influence on him.

Still, Mohandas' rebellion against adult authority continued. With another friend he tried smoking, which he knew his parents disapproved of. Since the boys had no money with which to buy cigarettes, they started to steal small coins.

Mohandas felt guilty about these forbidden pleasures. He soon gave them up, but his conscience kept bothering him. Finally he wrote out a confession to his father, admitting all of his sins except meat-eating. Knowledge of that, he believed, would be too much for his orthodox Hindu parents to bear. In his letter he promised faithfully never to repeat any of the sins.

Kaba Gandhi had fallen ill some weeks before this. When Mohandas finished writing his confession, he took it to his father's room.

Kaba sat up in bed and read the note while Mohandas watched. Tears began to trickle down the old man's face. For a minute he was still, his eyes closed. Then he tore up the letter and lay back on his pallet. Not a word did he say.

Mohandas, also weeping, stole quietly out of the room. His conscience was at peace at last. He had been honest with his father and he knew he had been forgiven.

3.   "English Gentleman"

For several months Kaba Gandhi was bedridden. Mohandas, who was now very close to his father, hurried home from school each day to nurse him. Daily he massaged his father's aching legs. Although his previous sins were never mentioned, Mohandas always felt that his confession had increased his father's love for him.

In 1885, when Mohandas was sixteen, Kaba Gandhi died, and Mohandas grieved deeply. Not long afterwards Mohandas became a father, but the baby lived only a few days, which added to Mohandas' sorrow.

Kaba left little wealth besides the gold necklace and amulet he had worn around his neck, but he bequeathed to his children a priceless heritage of honesty and integrity. Mohandas determined that Absolute Truth should be his life's goal, as it had been his father's.

In spite of the meagerness of Kaba's estate, the family members continued to live as they had, supported by the joint-family fund. Mohandas completed his studies at the high school and passed the college entrance examinations. Then he went alone to a college 100 miles east of Rajkot.

Mohandas was unhappy at college. All the courses were taught in English, and although he had studied English in high school he did not always understand what a professor was talking about. Besides, he was very lonely. He missed Kasturbai and his mother dreadfully. Still painfully shy, it was hard for him to make friends.

When Mohandas went home for vacation an old family friend, whom the Gandhi boys called Joshiji, came to call. Brothers and uncles assembled, as if for a family council.

Joshiji soon sensed that Mohandas wanted to drop out of school. "You must have a college education, Mohan," Joshiji insisted. "It is true that your father had little schooling, and still was able to hold a high post in government. But times have changed. A college degree is now necessary for advancement."

Both of Mohandas' brothers nodded solemnly. Neither of them had gone to college, but they were anxious for Mohandas to go. One of their father's sons should be able to succeed, in time, to his post as dewan of Rajkot.

"However," the family friend continued, "I do not agree that a college in India is the best place for our

Mohandas, right, and his older brother, Laxmidas, a short time before Mohan's departure for England

Mohan. If he is to be a dewan like his father and his grandfather before him, he should have a degree from an English college."

Mohandas caught his breath. Study in England! Such a thing had never occurred to him. And yet, now that it had been suggested, he knew it was precisely what he wanted to do. True, he would be far away from Kasturbai and his family, and he might have even more difficulty following lecture courses in an English college. But he would see the country that produced strong, brave Englishmen. He might find out how to develop these qualities himself.

"Yes," said Mohandas eagerly. "I want to go to England and study to be a doctor."

"A doctor!" protested his entire family. "That must never be!"

"Our father would never have agreed to a medical career for his son," Laxmidas objected. "The idea of studying dead bodies should be disgusting to a Hindu."

"It is out of the question," said his uncles.

"You must study law," Joshiji told Mohandas. "A degree in law will enable you to get a government post."

Much discussion followed. For days and weeks the Gandhi family considered, rejected, reconsidered, and finally accepted the plan of sending Mohandas, their youngest, to England for a three-year stay.

Putlibai had originally opposed the idea, but she gave her reluctant consent when Mohandas agreed to take a solemn oath to eat no meat, to drink no wine, and to be faithful to his marriage vows while he was away.

Mohandas was so anxious to go to England that he suggested selling his wife's jewelry to finance the trip. Hindu women traditionally wore many rich necklaces, bracelets, rings, and earrings. These often took the place of a family savings account, since they could be pawned or sold to raise money.

Kasturbai made no objection to her husband's suggestion of selling her valuable jewelry. A second child had recently been born to them, and she was absorbed in the care of their tiny son, Harilal. But Laxmidas, who was now secretary to the heir to the Porbandar throne, offered to finance his young brother's studies in England, and the jewelry was not sold.

In June, 1888, Mohandas bade good-bye to his mother, his wife, his baby son, and the rest of his relatives, and set out for Bombay. There he boarded a ship for England. He was not yet nineteen.

The ocean voyage proved to be an ordeal. Mohandas was not seasick, but he was too bashful to make friends with other passengers, or to ask waiters whether the dishes they served contained meat. In order to keep his vegetarian vow, he stopped going to the ship's

dining room and lived on sweets, nuts, and fruit for the entire three-week journey.

The ordeal did not end when the ship reached England. Mohandas, accustomed to loose thin clothing and light sandals, found English shirts and ties and long trousers and tight jackets irksome and ugly. He especially hated stockings and leather shoes.

Meals gave Mohandas even more trouble than dress. After using his fingers all his life, Mohandas found it awkward and difficult to eat with knife, fork, and spoon. Worse, it was almost impossible to find acceptable food. Everybody wanted him to eat meat. Hotel waiters, landladies, English friends, and Indians living in England—all pressed meat on him. They laughed at his vow of vegetarianism and urged him to forget it while in England.

To the son of Putlibai, however, a vow was sacred, never to be broken. This vow was especially important because it had been administered by his saintly mother.

Mohandas roamed the streets of London tirelessly, searching for a place where he could get appetizing vegetarian food. Sometimes he tramped ten or twelve miles in a day.

At last he found a vegetarian restaurant, and he had a good meal. There he made friends with other vegetarians, both Indians and Englishmen. He came across a book, *A Plea for Vegetarianism,* which he read with interest. It convinced him that vegetarianism was the best of all possible diets—healthful, economical, and spiritually uplifting. From that day on, Mohandas Gandhi was a vegetarian not merely because of a vow, but from choice and conviction.

Mohandas joined the Vegetarian Society of England. Its members were ultramodern intellectuals. Besides practicing vegetarianism, they believed in nonviolence and in the Simple Life. Mohandas became active in the work of the Society, and before long he was writing articles for its magazine.

Keeping the first part of his vow to his mother gave Mohandas no more trouble. He stopped eating in restaurants and boardinghouses, and did his own cooking. He learned to discipline his taste. He quit using spices, which he had been very fond of all his life—especially curry, ginger, cloves, and cinnamon. Soon he enjoyed the bland, natural tastes of vegetables.

"The real seat of the taste," he decided, "is not in the tongue but the mind."

The second part of his vow was easy to keep, because Mohandas did not drink wine or liquor. When he began his law studies at the Inns of Court, he found that this made him popular with his fellow students. In those days law students were required to eat six dinners together each term, and two bottles of wine were provided for each group of four. Since Mohandas

Gandhi as a law student in England

would not touch the wine, other students urged him to sit with them so they could have his share.

The third part of his vow led Mohandas into embarrassment. Soon after his arrival in London he learned that British marriage customs differed greatly from those in India. Child marriage was unknown. Mohandas, barely nineteen, was a husband and a father, and so were most of the Hindu students he met in London. Yet others behaved as if they were bachelors.

"Don't tell anybody you're married," his new Indian friends advised Mohandas. "It's easier to go out with English girls if they think you are single."

In spite of his decision after his father's death to make Absolute Truth his goal, Mohandas followed this dubious advice. On a holiday at the seashore he met a friendly old lady and allowed her to assume he was a bachelor. At once she began to promote a romance between him and the young lady who lived with her.

Mohandas enjoyed his visits with the Englishwomen, but his conscience bothered him. At last he wrote a letter to the old lady:

> Ever since we met at Brighton you have been kind to me. You have taken care of me even as a mother of her son. You also think that I should get married and . . . you have been introducing me to young ladies. Rather than allow matters to go further, I must confess to you that I have been unworthy of your affection. I should have told you when I began my visits to you that I was married . . . while yet a boy, and am the father of a son. . . .

The old lady readily forgave Mohandas. Their friendship continued, warmer than ever, now that there was frankness and openness between them. Mohandas never again tried to pass himself off as a bachelor, and he never again forgot that Truth is not Truth without complete frankness.

Many students from India tried to make themselves into English gentlemen. Mohandas tried too. He grew a mustache. He had new clothes made, including a top hat and an evening suit. He spent a lot of time before the mirror, brushing his stiff black hair and adjusting his tie. He invested in dancing lessons and elocution lessons, and he bought a violin and started to practice.

It took only a few months for Mohandas to decide that he did not want to be an English gentleman. He was an Indian, and an Indian he would remain. He sold his violin and stopped the dancing and elocution lessons. However, he continued to wear the fashionable English clothes.

Soon Mohandas found a new interest. When an Englishman questioned him about Hinduism, he discovered that he knew very little about it. So he began to study the *Bhagavad Gita*, or *Song of God*, which contains the basic principles of Hindu philosophy. Mohandas had heard parts of this beautiful poem all his life, but he had never thought about its meaning. Now the *Gita* gave him, for the first time, some definite religious convictions.

Then, at the urging of another friend, Mohandas began to read the Bible. He found the Old Testament difficult and confusing, but the story of Jesus' life and work in the New Testament appealed to him. When he came to the Sermon on the Mount his enthusiasm soared. Over and over Mohandas read these verses from Matthew:

> Resist not evil, but whosoever shall smite thee on thy right cheek, turn to him the other also. . . .
>
> And if any man . . . take away thy coat, let him have thy cloak also. . . .
>
> Love your enemies, bless them that curse you, do good to them that hate you, and pray for them which despite-fully use you and persecute you.

These words expressed the principles in the *Gita* that had so impressed Mohandas, those of nonviolence and returning good for evil.

Still Mohandas could not devote much time to religion because the study of law was his chief concern.

As he read English Common Law, Mohandas' understanding and appreciation of the British government steadily increased. Democracy, justice, and equality under the law were excellent principles. He wished that India could be a self-governing Dominion of the Empire, like Canada, instead of a British colony.

On June 10, 1891, Mohandas passed his bar examinations. He was now a lawyer. Two days later he sailed for India, after three long years away from home.

4. Failure in His Homeland

Laxmidas, Mohandas' eldest brother, was waiting at the dock in Bombay. He raised his hand to stop Mohandas' eager questions about the family.

"I have bad news, Mohan," he said soberly. "Ba is gone."

His mother dead? For Mohandas, it was as if the light of the world had gone out. Throughout his long stay abroad, he had looked forward to seeing Ba and telling her of all he had learned, all he had seen. His grief took the edge off his joy in seeing his wife and small son.

At 22, Kasturbai was prettier than before, a poised, competent young matron. Mohandas loved her more than ever, but he was still impatient with her, and sometimes unkind. Harilal, now nearly four, had grown into an active, intelligent little boy. Mohandas enjoyed playing with his son.

Mohandas tried to start a law practice in Bombay. He was a total failure as a trial lawyer, because his shyness prevented him from pleading a case. The first time he stood before the court, he simply could not force himself to say a word, and he had to hand the case over to someone else. He closed his office in Bombay and returned to Rajkot. Through the influence of his brother Laxmidas, he got work as a law secretary.

One day Laxmidas asked Mohandas to undertake a mission for him. During the time he was secretary to the heir to the throne of Porbandar, Laxmidas had been falsely accused of giving bad advice to his master. The British political agent, who was really the power behind the throne, had insisted on his dismissal. Now Laxmidas wanted Mohandas to help him regain that position.

"You met the British officer when he was in London on leave," Laxmidas reminded Mohandas. "Now that he has returned to India, I want you to go to him and put in a plea for me. Then I can regain my position at court."

Mohandas shook his head. "It would not be right to take advantage of such a slight acquaintance," he objected. "We scarcely knew each other. If the agent has been wrongly informed about you, why not submit a petition explaining matters? I will write it for you. Eventually you would receive justice."

"Justice!" snorted Laxmidas. "You know nothing of the world, Mohan. Here in India there is no justice. Influence is the only thing that counts. It is wrong for you to refuse to help your brother."

Painfully aware that his brother's generosity had made possible his law degree, Mohandas finally agreed.

Upon entering the Englishman's office, Mohandas met a cold, blank stare. He greeted the agent courteously and then he said, "We met last year in London. Perhaps you do not remember."

"I remember," the Englishman replied shortly.

Mohandas had heard that Englishmen, who might be very friendly with Indians while in England, changed completely when they returned to India. Now he saw that this was true. Quite obviously the English officer resented being reminded of the London acquaintance. Only later did Mohandas learn that the British, who were a minority ruling by force, did not dare allow a hint of friendliness or equality to creep into their relations with the subjugated Indians.

Having given his promise to Laxmidas, however, Mohandas brought up his case. He began to explain the situation that had caused his brother's dismissal from his court position.

The agent interrupted. "Your brother is an intriguer. If he has anything to say for himself, let him appeal through the proper channels. I will not listen to any more."

When Mohandas kept on with his defense of his brother, the officer rose impatiently.

"You must leave now," he commanded.

"Please let me finish," Mohandas said. "I have little more to say."

However, the Englishman would not listen to another word. He summoned his servant and had his caller thrown out of the house. Never in his life had Mohandas been so humiliated! To be manhandled as if he were a criminal or an Untouchable! He went home fuming, determined to sue the English officer.

Laxmidas persuaded Mohandas to forget the unhappy incident.

"Such things happen all the time," he said. "The British are autocratic rulers here in India, even in the native states. We have to submit to their tyranny and their snobbery; there is nothing else to do. If you are going to practice law in India, Mohan, you'll have to learn to take snubs and affronts from Englishmen. You must bribe them, flatter them, and court their favor."

For proud Mohandas K. Gandhi this advice was extremely distasteful. He could never fawn on anyone. Certainly he had no intention of trying to pacify the officer who had insulted him. Yet if he should attempt to practice law here, most of his work would come under the jurisdiction of that very man. So his career was doomed to failure from the beginning.

Mohandas still believed that British law and government were good, but the way the laws were administered in India was far from good. There was absolutely no "equality under the law" for Indians. The Indian National Congress had been organized a few years earlier, but it could not make laws or enforce them. All it did was to meet once a year and pass resolutions that seldom resulted in action.

Thoroughly depressed, Mohandas considered his unhappy situation. Day after day he performed his secretarial duties, played with his little boy, and tried to hide his unhappiness from Kasturbai. What, he wondered drearily, should he do?

One day Laxmidas showed him a letter from the business concern of Dada Abdulla and Company in Porbandar.

"We have business in South Africa," the letter said. "We now have a big case in the court there, a claim of 40,000 pounds." It was a big suit indeed, almost $200,000.

The letter said that the firm would like to send a man to South Africa to help the lawyers there with the case. They offered the job to Mohandas. He would be expected to remain in South Africa about a year. All his expenses would be paid, and he would be given a small salary.

Many Indians, Mohandas knew, had moved to South Africa. Some had gone as indentured workers in mines and plantations, others as merchants. He would not be a lone Indian in a strange land. Thankfully he accepted the offer. He was as anxious to leave India now as he had been to come home from England.

Mohandas' preparations were soon made. He bade farewell to his wife, his son Harilal, his brothers and uncles, and his new baby son Manilal.

Aware of tears in his own eyes and in Kasturbai's, he tried to be cheerful. "We will meet again in a year," he said.

Mohandas traveled to Bombay and boarded a ship for South Africa. It was April, 1893, and he was 23 years old.

5. "A Man of Color"

Wearing English clothes and a huge Indian turban, Mohandas Gandhi stood on the deck of the steamship as it docked in Durban, in the province of Natal, South Africa. He watched the milling throng on the wharf— white men, black men, and brown men. The whites elbowed Indians and blacks out of their path, and the dark-skinned people submitted meekly. This treatment of his fellow countrymen angered Gandhi. Even in India, few Englishmen were so rude!

When the gangplank was lowered, scores of Indians swarmed aboard to meet friends and relatives. Gandhi stood aloof.

Soon a large Indian in Muslim dress wearing an Arab turban approached him. He introduced himself as Abdulla Sheth, the South African partner of the Porbandar firm.

Abdulla surveyed Gandhi but there was no approval in his black eyes and no warmth in his formal greeting.

"Come with me," he directed shortly. "I will show you your room."

Gandhi soon learned that Abdulla was puzzled and

resentful because his partner had sent a man dressed like a wealthy European to South Africa. No doubt he expected to live like one.

Gandhi also sensed that Abdulla did not trust him, and was reluctant to send him to Pretoria where the lawsuit was being conducted. Pretoria was several hundred miles inland, in the province of the Transvaal.

Depressed, Gandhi wondered if he was to be a failure in South Africa too.

As time passed, however, the two men began to get acquainted. Abdulla's suspicions faded under the influence of Gandhi's honesty and frankness.

On Gandhi's third day in Durban, Abdulla took his guest to court with him. Gandhi could not understand why the English judge kept staring at him.

Finally, the magistrate spoke directly to Gandhi. "Remove your turban in this court."

Gandhi stared indignantly at the white-wigged judge. Why should he be singled out for such a command, when Abdulla and several others wore turbans?

"No, your honor," he replied.

"Then leave the courtroom," the judge ordered.

Gandhi rose and left the room. He wrote a letter of protest to the local newspaper.

When Abdulla joined him after court had adjourned, he explained to Gandhi that Arabs were permitted to wear turbans in court, but not Indians.

"You are an Indian," Gandhi countered, "yet you were allowed to keep your turban on."

Abdulla explained the complicated political situation in South Africa. Not only were there three skin colors—white, black, and brown—but each color had its restrictions, and its laws.

The Dutch, called Boers, had come first to South Africa as farmers and ranchers. Then the English came, drawn by the mineral wealth of the country—diamonds, gold, and coal. They drove the Dutch out of the southern provinces, and the Boers moved north to found the provinces of the Transvaal and the Orange Free State.

Although there was great rivalry and even hatred between the English and the Dutch, all whites were united in antagonism toward the blacks and the "colored," or brown people. The whites needed these other races to operate their mines and farm their plantations, but they feared them because they were so numerous. If they should ever unite, they could drive the white people out of South Africa.

Black people in South Africa outnumbered the whites by eighty to one, yet they had no status and no power. In the cities, blacks were forced to live in compounds and treated more like cattle than human beings.

The "colored" people were almost entirely Indian. English and Dutch merchants were jealous of the prosperous Indian merchants, and they were alarmed by the rapidly increasing Indian population.

The Indians in South Africa were disunited. They belonged to various castes, and each caste refused to associate with the others.

By far the largest group of Indians in South Africa was composed of indentured and freed laborers, many of whom were Untouchables. They had come to South Africa originally at the invitation of the British, who wanted cheap labor to work their sugar plantations and their mines. An indentured laborer signed an agreement to work for his South African employer for five years, almost as a slave. At the end of his term, he was free to get an independent job and settle down. These laborers were called "coolies," and Englishmen often labeled all Indians "coolie."

"I call myself an Arab," Abdulla told Gandhi, "because of my Islamic religion. Arabs may wear turbans in court, but 'coolie barristers,' as they will call you, are not permitted to."

By now Abdulla had begun to trust Gandhi, and he decided to send him to Pretoria to help with the lawsuit.

Transportation from Durban, in the British province of Natal, to Pretoria, in the Dutch province of Transvaal, was a roundabout, inconvenient, and complicated matter, involving three trains and two coaches. Gandhi bought a first-class ticket according to his custom and boarded the train for the first stage of his journey.

About 9 P.M. the train stopped at a town high in the mountains, and an Englishman entered the compartment. He glared at Gandhi, and then went away, returning a few minutes later with a railroad official.

"You must go to the third-class compartment," the officer told Gandhi.

"But I have a first-class ticket," Gandhi replied.

"That doesn't matter," the railroad official said. "Colored people are not permitted in this compartment."

Humiliated and angry, Gandhi refused to leave his compartment. He was pushed out of the train, and it steamed off. He was left standing on the platform in a strange town late at night. It was midwinter, because the seasons are reversed south of the equator.

All night long Gandhi huddled in the drafty, dark waiting room. Gandhi's overcoat had been packed in his luggage, which the hostile railroad official held. So he sat and shivered and thought.

Should he take the next train back to Durban and the first ship to India? The temptation was almost irresistible. Why remain in a country where white men went out of their way to intimidate and humiliate a person of another color? In India, although the British never let anyone forget their power, an educated Indian was seldom insulted. . . . Of course, there was the

English agent whom he had approached on his brother's behalf; if he returned to India, he would have to humble himself to that officer.

Should he, then, go on to Pretoria as he had promised Abdulla, and do the work he had come to South Africa to do? If he followed that course, again he would have to pocket his pride; he would have to allow insults to slide past him, unprotested.

Discouraged and depressed, Gandhi thought wryly that no matter which course he chose, he would have to humble himself. Neither course of action pleased him. Both would be negative, rather than positive. Actually, the insults were merely a symptom of a deep-seated disease: color prejudice. He wasn't the only Indian to be insulted and discriminated against, he realized now. Such things were common occurrences for Indians in South Africa. The only difference between him and his fellow countrymen was that they had learned to accept injustices philosophically.

As morning dawned, Gandhi came to a momentous decision: he would not run away; he would stay in South Africa until he had accomplished his mission. On the other hand, he would not submit meekly to discrimination; he would work to wipe out color prejudice in South Africa.

As soon as he arrived in Pretoria he settled himself in a boardinghouse and began to learn the details of

Abdulla's lawsuit. Then Gandhi called a meeting of all the Indians in Pretoria. To this group he made his first public speech. He was so earnest that his customary shyness did not bother him.

"My fellow countrymen," Gandhi began in his thin, high-pitched voice. "I would like you to consider with me your situation here in the Transvaal." He proceeded to list the ways in which the Dutch prevented them from becoming first-class citizens. Indians were not permitted to vote, to own land, or even to live anywhere except in certain slum areas. Indians were forbidden to travel in first-class railroad compartments, stay in European hotels, or eat in restaurants patronized by white men. They could not travel from one province of South Africa to another without a permit. There were certain streets in Pretoria which they could not use. After nine o'clock at night they could not be on the streets at all.

The list went on and on. The audience listened intently, frequently nodding agreement.

Then Gandhi began to outline a plan designed to better the situation of the Indians in South Africa.

"Part of our sad condition stems from our own actions," he told his listeners. "Europeans say, with some truth, that Indians have dirty, unsanitary habits. They say we cannot be trusted to tell the truth. They say we cannot communicate with them, or even at times with each other."

Gandhi suggested a five-point program to overcome these objections. He urged his fellow countrymen:

1. ALWAYS TELL THE TRUTH, EVEN IN BUSINESS. Let us get the reputation of being honest and dependable. Then Europeans will be glad to have us as residents, and they will want to do business with us.

2. ADOPT MORE SANITARY HABITS. Keep your homes as clean as you keep your person. Learn from the Europeans how to dispose of wastes.

3. LEARN ENGLISH. There are so many different languages in India that many of us cannot converse together. We must all learn a common language, and I advise English.

4. FORGET CASTE AND RELIGIOUS DIFFERENCES. Let us all work together—Hindus, Muslims, Parsis, and Christians; high castes and low castes; indentured laborers and free. Then we can grow strong enough to make our influence felt.

5. FORM AN ASSOCIATION TO INFORM THE AUTHORITIES OF OUR HARDSHIPS.

The meeting was a great success. So encouraged—

even inspired—were the Pretorian Indians that they formed the suggested organization then and there.

While the lawsuit dragged on, Gandhi made a study of the social, economic, and political situation of Indians in South Africa. He learned that discrimination by the British was less extreme than that of the Boers. Because England ruled India, all Indians were supposed to be citizens of the British Empire, and therefore under the protection of the Crown no matter where they lived. Just the same, the British were as anxious to get rid of the Indians as were the Dutch. Both governments passed oppressive laws designed to stop Indian immigration, to discourage Indian merchants and free workers, and to drive them back to India. Indians were wanted in South Africa only as indentured servants.

After Gandhi had been in Pretoria for a year he persuaded both parties of the lawsuit to submit their grievances to arbitration; representatives of both sides met with an impartial third party. Eventually they arrived at a compromise agreement, and everyone was pleased. Gandhi saw that arbitration was a way of settling quarrels, out of court, without bitterness.

His work in South Africa was now finished, he thought. He returned to Durban and prepared to sail for India.

6. A Long Fight Begins

Abdulla was extremely grateful for Gandhi's help in bringing about a satisfactory settlement of the lawsuit. He gave a day-long farewell party for him, and invited a number of influential Muslims.

During the afternoon Gandhi happened to see some English newspapers. As he turned the pages of the *Natal Mercury* a headline caught his eye: INDIAN FRANCHISE. He read the story with ever growing indignation.

"Have you seen this, Abdulla?" he asked. "Did you know about this franchise bill?"

His host shook his head. "I never read the English papers," he replied.

"Surely," Gandhi exclaimed, looking around at the guests, "some of you knew about this bill now before the Natal legislature. The British mean to deprive all Indians here of the right to vote!"

The guests had known nothing of the bill, and nobody seemed to see its significance.

One of the men said, "What does it matter whether we can vote or not? We can never hold office."

"Holding office is not the point," Gandhi said. "It's the principle of the thing. If this bill passes, all Natal Indians will be like our countrymen under the Dutch government of the Transvaal and Orange Free State, unable to vote."

The merchants looked at each other. One by one they nodded. "What can be done about it?" asked Abdulla.

One of the guests spoke up. "I'll tell you what can be done. You must keep Gandhi here, Abdulla, instead of letting him return to India. Keep him for another month, and we'll fight this bill under his direction."

Everyone agreed enthusiastically.

Money and manpower for the campaign were quickly promised, and the farewell party became a work party.

In spite of the vigorous efforts of Gandhi and his co-workers, the legislature passed the bill. Then Gandhi drew up a petition to be submitted to Queen Victoria's Colonial Secretary, urging his veto of the bill. In two weeks time 10,000 signatures were obtained.

The month that Gandhi promised passed swiftly. His Indian friends urged him to settle in Natal permanently.

"If I were to remain, I would need money to live on," Gandhi replied. "I'd have to find work as a lawyer."

About twenty Indian merchants immediately hired Gandhi as lawyer for their firms, so that he was assured of an adequate income. He rented a house in Natal which quickly became headquarters for the campaign

Attorney Monhandas K. Gandhi, center, and staff in his Johannesburg law office. Gandhi spent twenty years in South Africa fighting for the rights of Indians.

for Indian rights, and a refuge for anyone in need of help.

In order to practice law, Gandhi would need approval to appear before the Supreme Court, so he filed an application—the first "colored" man to do so. The Law Society of Natal promptly opposed his application, but the judge ruled in Gandhi's favor.

As soon as he had been sworn in, the chief justice said, "Now, Mr. Gandhi, take off your turban. As a practicing attorney, you must submit to the rules of the court."

Gandhi still felt that the order was unjust, but he removed his turban.

In 1894 a new tax bill was passed by the Natal legislature. It required an indentured laborer, who had worked out his term and wanted to remain in South Africa as a free worker, to pay an annual tax of three pounds for himself and for each member of his family. Laborers could never afford such a tax, since it took them six months to earn three pounds. The law was a device to force Indians to return to India—even those born in South Africa.

When Gandhi had been in South Africa three years, he saw that wiping out color prejudice was going to take time. He returned to India to get his family.

Gandhi spent most of his time in India making speeches about the poor conditions in South Africa.

In December, 1896, he returned to Durban with his wife, his two sons, and his sister's son.

Gandhi stood at the rail of the steamship *Courland* as it crept into the harbor, with the steamer *Naderi* alongside. The two ships held about 800 Indians. Many of them, like him, were returning to their homes in South Africa.

Gandhi's sons and his nephew stood beside him. His wife, Kasturbai, waited modestly in the background, as was proper.

"Why do we have to wear these funny clothes, Papa?" asked four-year-old Manilal.

"I hate these heavy shoes and stockings," eight-year-old Harilal grumbled.

Gandhi looked down proudly at the little boys. They looked well-dressed, he thought, in their long coats and trousers.

"My family must set an example for other Indians," he said, "and also uphold my prestige among Europeans."

Because there had been an epidemic of the bubonic plague in Bombay when the ships sailed, the *Courland* and the *Naderi* were put under quarantine and passengers were not permitted to land.

Gandhi soon learned that there was more behind the quarantine than fear of plague. Every day his friend Abdulla sent him news of the city, and the news was not good. Distorted versions of the speeches Gandhi had made throughout India had been printed in the Natal press. His supposed statements had aroused the anger of English citizens, who also accused him of bringing two shiploads of new Indian immigrants into South Africa. There were rumors that if Gandhi dared to land, he would be lynched.

The quarantine dragged on. Finally, on January 13, 1897, it was lifted and passengers were allowed to land. At once a crowd began to gather around the dock. Gandhi knew they were waiting for him. He sent his family in a carriage to the home of a wealthy Indian friend, the merchant Rustomji, so they would not be in danger if a mob attacked him.

While others were going ashore, a reporter from the *Natal Advertiser* came aboard the *Courland*. He began to ask Gandhi questions about his speeches in India.

Fortunately Gandhi had kept copies of all the speeches he had made in India, and he gave them to the reporter. He pointed out that he had said nothing in India that he had not already said hundreds of times during the three years he lived in Natal. He also informed the reporter that many of the passengers on the two ships were old residents rather than new immigrants. In any case he himself had had nothing whatever to do with bringing any of the Indian passengers to Natal. The reporter promised to print all this in the next day's paper.

At about 4:30 Gandhi walked down the gangplank with an English friend. They set out on foot for the house of Rustomji Sheth, two miles away.

The crowd, though large, seemed peaceable, and Gandhi's spirits lightened.

Suddenly some small English boys recognized him and began to shout, "Gandhi! Gandhi!" They picked up pebbles and pelted him. Half a dozen men ran toward them and began throwing rocks.

"We'll take a rickshaw," said Gandhi's friend, "and get out of this crowd quickly." He signaled a Zulu rickshaw boy. But the hoodlums would not let Gandhi get into the vehicle. They set upon him, pulled off his turban, and began to beat him.

More and more men joined the boys in tormenting Gandhi; he recognized several as leaders in the British community. They pulled Gandhi's friend away so he could not help him. With shrieks and screams they slapped Gandhi and beat and kicked him. They pelted him with stones, bricks, and rotten eggs.

Gandhi felt himself fainting and he caught hold of the railing of a house. He clung there, wavering, trying desperately to get his breath. But the rioters gave him no rest. They fell on him with renewed fury and drove him on down the street.

Suddenly a woman's indignant voice rose above the shouts and curses of the mob. "What is going on here?"

Through a fog of faintness and terrible pain, Gandhi recognized Mrs. Alexander, wife of the police superintendent of Durban. She carried a parasol.

"Why, it's Mr. Gandhi!" Mrs. Alexander exclaimed. "You cowards! You're killing him! Stop it! Stop!"

Her words had no effect on the rioters. Their attacks on Gandhi's frail body continued. With no hesitation, Mrs. Alexander stepped close to him, opened her parasol, and held it over him. She walked along beside him, keeping herself between him and the hoodlums. Now they could not hit Gandhi without hurting her, and no one in Natal would dare harm a white woman, especially the wife of the police chief. Uncertain, Gandhi's attackers fell back.

Then the clatter of hoofs was heard. Someone had called the police. A mounted posse rode up, with orders to escort Gandhi to safety.

The police chief and his posse accompanied Gandhi to Mr. Rustomji's house, where he rejoined his family. A doctor came and treated Gandhi's wounds; fortunately, none was serious, but he was weary and sore.

Soon he heard a growing tumult outside the house. The white mob had followed him.

A shout arose. "We want Gandhi! We'll burn down this house unless you deliver Gandhi to us!"

Mr. Alexander went outside. When he saw the size of the mob—thousands where he had expected only hundreds—he held a hushed conference with his detectives. Quickly they made plans. The police chief sent some detectives back inside the house, and then he climbed on a bench in front of the door. He began to talk to the rioters to distract their attention.

Meanwhile, the detectives had reported to Gandhi, "The chief says you are to disguise yourself as an Indian constable and escape from the house at once."

Gandhi did not need the urging of Kasturbai and Rustomji to obey the police chief; he knew Mr. Alexander would not send such instructions unless the situation was desperate.

An Indian constable, a member of the posse, gave Gandhi his uniform. Two detectives painted their faces brown and dressed like Indian merchants.

When everything was ready the men went out through merchant Rustomji's warehouse. They slipped through the mob unnoticed, because everybody was watching Mr. Alexander and singing with him:

Hang old Gandhi
On a sour apple tree. . . .

The rioters roared for more, and the police chief began another verse. Gandhi and the detectives sneaked down a by-lane, through a shop, and to a carriage that Mr. Alexander had sent to the end of the street to wait for them. At last Gandhi reached the police station and the superintendent was notified of his safety.

An hour later Mr. Alexander and the rest of his posse returned to the station.

"The crowd did not believe me when I told them you were not in the house," he reported. "So I asked them to choose a committee to make a search. I made them promise that if the committee did not find you, they would return peacefully to their homes. The people kept their word, and the city is now quiet."

The next morning the citizens of Durban read in the *Natal Advertiser* Gandhi's defense of his conduct in India. Fair-minded Englishmen realized that he had done nothing underhanded or harmful. Most people who had joined in the attack on him now regretted it.

They regretted it even more when they learned that Gandhi, true to his principles of nonviolence and returning good for evil, refused to identify his attackers.

"I forgive them," Gandhi told the government representative who questioned him. "They were misled. The government of Natal was at fault. While my ship lay at anchor, there was plenty of time for an investigation of the charges against me. If you had published your findings, there would have been no mob."

Gandhi's behavior during the attempted lynching, and his generous attitude afterward, earned him the respect, and even friendship, of many Englishmen.

7. The Peaceful Fighter

Gandhi's family soon settled into their new life. Instead of sending his boys to school, Gandhi taught them himself at home. They could have attended the schools for European children, because of the respect Gandhi had earned from the English colony. However, other Indian children were not admitted to these schools, and Gandhi would not accept for his own family what was denied to others.

Gandhi's home-teaching was not entirely successful. Although he had unlimited patience with his clerks, his co-workers, and his followers, he had little patience with members of his own family, as Kasturbai had learned as a child-bride. Besides, his law practice and his public life kept him increasingly busy, so the school lessons were irregular. The boys came to resent their lack of proper education.

Kasturbai too had reason for resentment. Gandhi could not forget his superiority to his wife in education. He continually told her what to do, what to cook, how to cook it, how to eat (with knives and forks, not fingers), how to dress, how the laundry should be done and the house cleaned, and how to manage the boys. Kasturbai often had trouble hiding her indignation. Occasionally, she defied him openly.

Another thing that made Kasturbai angry was her husband's refusal to hire enough servants. His law practice now brought in an annual income of more than 5,000 pounds, or about $25,000. Kasturbai believed that they should have several servants and live in comfort. But Gandhi refused. Most of his money was used to fight against color prejudice and to assist the many Indians who came to him for help. A share also went to Laxmidas in India for the joint-family fund.

Besides, Gandhi had come to believe that people should not depend on servants, but should take care of themselves and live simply with few possessions. He expected his family, his numerous law clerks, friends, and the people he took in who needed help, to wait on themselves. Only temporary guests and new residents were entitled to any service, he said.

The Gandhi house, built in the Western style, had no running water and no plumbing. Each bedroom had a chamber pot, which had to be emptied daily. To caste-conscious Kasturbai, this was work for an Untouchable, but her husband refused to hire an Untouchable "sweeper."

"We must remove the curse of Untouchability,"

Gandhi insisted. "Until we Indians shake off our prejudice toward the Untouchables who make up one-fifth of our nation, we cannot expect the English to rid themselves of their color prejudice toward us."

Kasturbai was not convinced.

One day Gandhi brought home a guest and a new law clerk. The clerk was a Christian, the son of Untouchables.

"For a few days, until he becomes accustomed to our ways," Gandhi told his wife, "we will attend to his bedroom. You will clean his chamber pot and I will clean that of our other guest."

"No!" said Kasturbai. "The man is an Untouchable. I will have nothing to do with him or anything that belongs to him."

"Very well," said Gandhi. "I will empty his pot and you can take care of the guest's."

"No!" Kasturbai repeated. "That is just as bad. You will be polluted, and you will not cleanse yourself as a good Hindu should."

Gandhi's temper rose. "I am the master here!" he stormed. "You will empty that chamber pot and you will do it now!"

Crying bitterly, Kasturbai climbed the steep, narrow outside stairs to the room of the Untouchable clerk. She brought the pot down, still weeping.

Gandhi, waiting at the foot of the stairs, scolded her.

"Why are you making such a fuss? Stop that foolish crying."

Kasturbai turned on him furiously. "Are you not satisfied? I am obeying your cruel, stupid commands."

"No!" Gandhi retorted. "I am not satisfied. It is not enough to do a service for someone grudgingly. You must do it cheerfully."

But Kasturbai continued to weep, and Gandhi's self-control snapped. "I will not have this nonsense in my house!" he raged, grabbing her arm roughly.

"Keep your house to yourself, then," she shouted back, trying to pull away from him. "Let me go!"

Gandhi, really beside himself now, pulled his wife to the gate and started to push her out into the street.

Still sobbing wildly, Kasturbai appealed to his pride. "Have you no sense of shame? For heaven's sake, shut the gate and stop acting as if I were your slave."

Slowly Gandhi's anger died and he realized that he had been behaving badly. He led Kasturbai gently back into the house. But he did not relent on the question of emptying the chamber pots. Eventually she obeyed him.

In 1899 war broke out between the British and the Dutch, both of whom wanted to control all of South Africa. Gandhi announced that he would form an ambulance corps to help the British. Ever since he had nursed his dying father, he had been interested in nursing and doctoring. For the past few years he had devoted two hours a day to helping out in a charity hospital in Durban maintained by the wealthy merchant Rustomji.

Other Indians protested against helping the British. "They are our enemies, not our friends!" they said.

"We are citizens of the British Empire," Gandhi reminded them. "We are asking for equality under its laws, so it is our duty to help the Empire."

More than a thousand Indians, including 800 indentured laborers, volunteered for the ambulance corps. Throughout the Boer War they nursed wounded soldiers on battlefields and in hospitals.

The war ended in 1901. The victorious British now ruled all of South Africa, but they gave the Boers a voice in the government. Gandhi and other leaders of the Indian Ambulance Corps were awarded medals for their contribution to the war effort.

Gandhi believed that the Indians' war work would also be rewarded by repeal of the discriminatory laws, and he decided his work in South Africa was finished. He would return to India to live.

The Indian community of Durban gave a lavish farewell party for Gandhi, their Indian rights champion. Rich gifts were bestowed on him: gold, silver, and diamond ornaments, including a solid gold necklace for Kasturbai.

That night, after the party, Gandhi could not sleep. Wealth had no place in the life he planned, a life of service and voluntary poverty. Why then should he keep this expensive jewelry?

Sleepless, Gandhi paced up and down his room. By morning, he had come to a decision. He wrote a letter setting up a public trust fund with the jewelry. He named his friend, Mr. Rustomji, administrator of the fund, which was to be used for Indians in need.

Before telling Kasturbai what he had done, Gandhi persuaded his older sons to support his decision if their mother objected to it. Two more sons, Ramdas and Devadas, had been born to the Gandhis during their five years in South Africa, but they were too young to be consulted in this matter.

Kasturbai did indeed object to Gandhi's proposal. "Give up that valuable gold necklace?" she protested. "Certainly not! I would never dare to wear it, after all you have said about women's foolish habit of wearing jewelry, but I shall certainly not give it away."

"Why do you wish to keep it, if you won't wear it?" Gandhi asked reasonably.

"For my daughters-in-law," Kasturbai replied.

"The boys aren't married yet," her husband pointed out. "It will be years before our sons marry, for I will not allow any child marriages in my family. Besides, I would never choose brides who are fond of jewelry."

For an hour they argued, but neither could convince the other. At last Gandhi said flatly, "We will say no more. I am putting the jewels in a public trust fund, and I will not allow you to keep a single thing."

Kasturbai had no choice but to accept her husband's decision.

Gandhi and his family sailed for India in 1901, but he agreed to return to Africa if his presence was considered essential in the work against color prejudice.

Very soon indeed he was summoned back. The discriminatory laws had not been repealed, and others were being proposed. In 1902 he returned to South Africa and opened another law office, this time in Johannesburg in the Transvaal. Again he took up the fight for equal rights for Indians.

In 1903 Gandhi started a weekly newspaper in Natal, which he called *Indian Opinion.* He hired an editor to manage it, but he himself wrote most of the copy and paid the expenses of the paper; sometimes it cost $300 a month. He decided to go to Natal and find some way to publish the paper more economically.

During the train journey to Natal Gandhi read a book that a friend had given him, *Unto This Last,* by John Ruskin, an Englishman. The book fascinated Gandhi. It strengthened his belief in voluntary poverty and the Simple Life that he had absorbed from the *Gita* and the Sermon on the Mount. By the time the train arrived in Durban, Gandhi was ready to put his principles into practice.

"I will set up a community farm," he decided, "and move the presses of *Indian Opinion* there. Everyone will work on the farm, and help out on the presses. Each one will draw the same small living wage. We will live as simply as possible, like one big family."

Within a week Gandhi had bought 100 acres of land at Phoenix, near Durban. The property had a spring, many fruit trees, and a dilapidated cottage. Mr. Rustomji donated building material, and Gandhi and his helpers erected a big shed for the printing press. They also built eight simple cottages. Since the place had long been uninhabited and the land was overgrown with grass and weeds, poisonous snakes were a constant menace. But Gandhi, believing firmly in ahimsa, or nonviolence, would not allow a single snake to be killed.

"The snakes will not harm us if we don't harm them," he declared confidently. And strangely, they never did.

Besides newspaper press workers, half a dozen families, both European and Indian, settled at Phoenix Farm. Each settler was given three acres of land to live on and to farm. Gandhi had his share. In his house he built a shower; it was made of a watering can set in the roof, which sprinkled water on him when he pulled a string.

Much as he wanted to, Gandhi could not remain long at Phoenix Farm because it was too far from his law office. Since the project required money, he returned to Johannesburg to earn it.

Although he could not live at Phoenix, Gandhi determined to live a Simple Life, as far as possible, in Johannesburg. He discarded much of his furniture and after that all of his family and guests sat cross-legged on mats to eat. This was no hardship for those who had grown up in India, but European guests found it difficult.

Instead of buying baker's bread, the Gandhi household began to make its own. Gandhi bought a heavy iron hand mill, and the various members of the household, including children and guests, took turns grinding the flour.

Gandhi employed one servant, who was treated as a member of the family. The older children helped him in his work, even cleaning chamber pots and toilets.

Gandhi persuaded his family to wash their own clothes, setting the example himself. On his first attempt at laundering a shirt, he used far too much starch and appeared in court with his shirt shedding white flakes like a small snowstorm. Gandhi joined in the laugh on himself, but he did not give up his attempts at laundering.

When a white barber refused to cut his hair, Gandhi

cut it himself. The result was a patchwork of too-short and too-long hair, which amused his friends. But Gandhi did not care. He felt that he was making progress toward the Simple Life.

Another thing Gandhi's friends laughed at was his obsession with cleanliness and sanitation. He never stopped urging his fellow Indians to keep their toilets clean, and their garbage picked up. Some of his friends fondly called him, "The Great Scavenger."

Gandhi's fads did not always amuse his family. He went from one food fad to another, trying to find an ideal diet. He believed that a person's food has a lot to do with his self-control, and he wanted to discipline himself completely. He gave up eating cereals, then milk, then nuts. He tried living entirely on fruits, then solely on nuts with a little lemon juice added. When ill, he no longer took medicines. Instead, he experimented with earth poultices and water treatments. He did not always insist on his family joining him in his experiments, but sometimes they felt obliged to.

Soon Gandhi began to fast occasionally, to take no food at all for a day or two at a time. He discovered that his mother had been right when she told him fasting helps a person to concentrate on spiritual matters, and thus to become more saintly.

Then Gandhi carried self-control and non-possession to an extreme. He announced to his family one day,

"My wife and my children should be no more important to me than anyone else. The whole of mankind should be my family. From now on, my sons will have nothing from me that I cannot give to all children, and I will live with my wife as though we were brother and sister."

No one objected. Kasturbai and his sons had long felt that Gandhi had more concern for the rest of the Indian people than he had for his own family. Sometimes his sons envied boys who were not related to Papa, for he could be so amusing, patient, and kind with other people's children.

8. Prisoners for a Principle

On August 22, 1906, Gandhi read in the *Transvaal Gazette* a shocking article. An ordinance, called the "Black Act," had been proposed in the Transvaal legislature. It would require every Indian man, woman, and child over the age of eight to register and be fingerprinted. If a person did not register, he could be deported. Also, each Indian must have a certificate, to be carried at all times. If his certificate was not produced on demand, the person could be fined, imprisoned, and deported.

Policemen and government agents were to be free to stop any Indian, anywhere, any time, and demand to see his certificate. They could also enter any Indian home without permission for the same purpose. Since Indian women were kept in seclusion and were not to be seen by men, the prospect of European men entering their homes at will was dreadful.

"This is terrible!" Gandhi exclaimed to Kasturbai.

"It would be better to die than to submit to such a degrading law! Something must be done."

Gandhi remembered what Kasturbai, as a child-bride, had taught him about passive resistance. He also recalled a book he had read during his first year in South Africa, *The Kingdom of God Is Within You.* The Russian author, Leo Tolstoy, advocated nonviolence, which Gandhi had known all his life as ahimsa. However, there was a difference. In Hindu philosophy ahimsa was a gentle, negative practice of refraining from harm to humans and animals, but Tolstoy believed nonviolence could become a strong, positive course of action. Nonviolence, Tolstoy said, could even convert a misguided ruling class. Gandhi decided to try it out.

On September 11, at Gandhi's summons, more than 3,000 Indians met in the Imperial Theater in Johannesburg. Rich and poor, merchants, lawyers, indentured laborers, servants, waiters—representatives of many trades and many faiths—all assembled in the big theater. Every seat, from orchestra circle to balcony, was filled.

Gandhi told the crowd what the "Black Act" would mean to them. He read a resolution he had drafted, and then he explained it.

"We will launch a passive resistance campaign," he said. "We will refuse to obey the law, if it passes."

Then he pointed out the possible consequences of such disobedience.

> We might have to go to jail, where we might be insulted. We might have to go hungry and suffer extreme heat or cold. Hard labor might be imposed upon us. We might be flogged. . . . We might be fined heavily and our property might be attached. . . . Opulent today we might be reduced to abject poverty tomorrow. We might be deported. Suffering from starvation and similar hardships in jail, some of us might fall ill and even die. . . . But I can boldly declare, and with certainty, that so long as there is even a handful of men true to their pledge, there can only be one end to the struggle, and that is victory.

The great audience listened respectfully. When Gandhi finished speaking, a solemn hush filled the theater.

Then the vote was called for. Every person in the great hall rose, and 3,000 hands were raised.

"I swear," repeated 3,000 voices solemnly, "in the name of God, that I will not obey this ordinance if it becomes law, and I will refrain from violence." The first passive resistance movement had been launched.

However, Gandhi did not like the term "passive resistance." To him there was nothing passive in resisting evil. Eventually he coined a new name, *satyagraha,* meaning the force born of truth and love.

Gandhi now began to educate his people through his newspaper, *Indian Opinion.* Several issues were devoted to passive resistance.

"Satyagraha," Gandhi wrote, "is not merely resistance to evil. It is the positive action of doing good. It is putting into practice the principles taught in the *Gita* and in the Sermon on the Mount. 'Love your enemies, do good to those that hate you, pray for those that despitefully use you.' Satyagraha hates the evil deed but has only love for the doer of the deed. We will overcome our enemies with love, not with hate or violence. We will convert them from wrong-doing to right-doing."

When the Black Act went into effect in July, 1907, Gandhi and his people were ready. Indians refused to register and picketed the registry office. Peaceably they tried to dissuade others from registering, and in most cases they succeeded. Very few Indians obeyed the hated law.

Soon many prominent residents of the Indian community, including Gandhi, received official notices that they must either register or leave the Transvaal. They did neither.

On January 11, 1908, Gandhi and about twenty other people were arrested and taken to court. Gandhi had often appeared in that court as a lawyer; today he stood in the dock, a prisoner. But he did not waver. He smiled impartially at his fellow prisoners and at the bewigged, stern-faced judge.

"I am the leader of this disobedience movement," he told the magistrate when he was allowed to speak. "As such, I deserve the heaviest sentence. I beg you to sentence me to hard labor."

The judge sentenced Gandhi, like the others, to two months imprisonment without hard labor.

In spite of the bad food, the dirty prison clothes he had to wear, and the overcrowded condition of the jail, Gandhi rather enjoyed prison. It gave him a much needed rest. He had plenty of time to read. He taught a fellow prisoner English. He kept notes on the number of satyagrahis who were arrested; at one time there were 150 in a single cell. This told Gandhi that his followers were holding fast to their vows, and he was pleased.

When Gandhi had been in prison two weeks, the former Boer general, Jan Christian Smuts, now minister of finance and defense in the Transvaal, sent for him. After a long talk, the two came to an agreement.

Gandhi promised that the Indians would register voluntarily, and the general promised that if they did, he would have the compulsory registration law repealed.

Gandhi kept his side of the bargain. He himself was the first to register, and through the pages of *Indian Opinion* he urged his fellow countrymen to do so, too.

General Smuts, on the other hand, did not keep his promise. The Black Act was not repealed.

After consulting with his associates, Gandhi sent a letter to General Smuts. He told him that unless the Black Act was repealed by 2 P.M. on August 16, the certificates the Indians had received through voluntary registration would be burned.

By four o'clock on August 16 a great mass of Indians had gathered on the grounds of the Hamidia Mosque in Johannesburg. Indians of all classes sat cross-legged on the ground, filling every foot of available space. On a platform stood an immense four-footed iron cauldron and a can of paraffin.

As the meeting was called to order, a messenger rode up on a bicycle. He handed Gandhi a telegram.

"This is from General Smuts," Gandhi announced, and he read the message aloud. General Smuts regretted the decision to burn the certificates, but he intended to enforce the law, regardless.

The great throng cheered, as if they welcomed another opportunity for passive resistance to the Black

Act. The resolution to burn the certificates was then adopted, and about 2,000 certificates were collected from the crowd and thrown into the huge kettle.

"By burning our certificates," Gandhi explained to the people, "we declare our solemn resolution never to submit to the Black Act. If any of you have changed your mind about this step, come forward and reclaim your certificate."

"We do not want them back!" the crowd shouted. "Burn the certificates!"

At a signal, the certificates were sprinkled with paraffin and then set ablaze. As one man, the assembled Indians rose to their feet and cheered while watching the crackling flames leap high.

When the fire had died to ashes, all present stood silent for a long minute, as if they were praying.

An English newspaper reporter who witnessed the scene reported later, "This act by the Transvaal Indians is comparable to that of the American colonists when they staged the Boston Tea Party nearly a century and a half ago."

9.   The Great March

Burning the voluntary certificates did not persuade the government to repeal the Black Act. On the contrary, General Smuts announced his determination to make the newly formed Union of South Africa "a white man's country":

> However difficult this task may be we have put our foot down, and we will keep it there. We will eradicate the Asiatic cancer which has already eaten so deeply into the vitals of South Africa.

Gandhi wrote to General Smuts, announcing plans for another passive resistance movement.

The laws that Indians resented most, besides the Black Act, were the crushing three-pound tax on former indentured laborers and the lack of voting privileges. But these laws would be difficult to defy with passive resistance, so Gandhi urged the Indians to disobey other laws.

At once hundreds began to travel from one province to another without the required permits. Hundreds more sold goods without licenses. Thousands went out on the streets after 9 P.M. and walked on paths and streets that were forbidden to Asiatics.

As Gandhi had expected, the government had these lawbreakers arrested, and the jails were soon overflowing. Some Indians, including Gandhi's eldest son Harilal, served four or five jail terms in succession.

Gandhi himself was jailed again. This time his request for hard labor was granted, and his health nearly broke under harsh treatment and backbreaking work.

In spite of the way he was treated, Gandhi's spirit remained strong. His cheerfulness, his ready wit, and his never-failing love for mankind never faltered. Eventually he was released from jail and resumed the fight.

Five years of struggle followed. The strain began to tell on Gandhi's followers. Some weakened and went back on their vows. Gandhi regretted their weakness but he did not criticize or condemn them.

Caring for the families of satyagrahis who were serving jail sentences became a big problem. It was solved at last, in May, 1910, by a friend of Gandhi's who bought 1,100 acres of land near Johannesburg and gave it to the satyagraha organization. Gandhi named the place Tolstoy Farm. It had 1,000 fruit trees, a spring, two wells, and a house. Other houses were soon built, and Gandhi moved his family there as well as the families of satyagrahis who were in prison.

At first about 75 men, women, and children lived at Tolstoy Farm: Hindus, Muslims, Parsis, Chinese, and Christians. More came later. The residents spoke half a dozen languages. Community cooking and eating were customary. While vegetarianism was not insisted on, Gandhi made his wishes so plain that soon nobody asked for meat.

There were no chairs at the farm, and no beds. Everybody slept on the ground, in the open when weather permitted. Anyone who had to go to the city on business could take the bus, but anyone who went for pleasure was obliged to walk. Gandhi sometimes walked the 21 miles to his law office and back again in the same day; all his life he took long brisk walks daily.

There were no servants at Tolstoy Farm. Gandhi was general manager, sanitation supervisor, sandal-maker, and head schoolmaster. He also acted as baker, and he learned to make orange marmalade. Praise of his bread or marmalade pleased him far more than a fat fee for a law case.

Twice during these years Gandhi traveled to England to lobby against anti-Indian laws. Each time he returned without having accomplished his aim. Each time he returned a little more disillusioned with the British Empire.

In March, 1913, an appalling announcement was made. The Supreme Court had ruled that only Christian marriages were legal in South Africa. This meant that the marriages of all Hindus, Muslims, and Parsis were invalid!

So great was the general indignation at this new blow that Indians rushed to Gandhi from all over South Africa to volunteer for satyagraha. Women joined the movement for the first time, giving up their traditional seclusion.

Quickly Gandhi laid out his strategy and organized his "army." A group of women was directed to cross illegally from the Transvaal province into Natal, and in this way court arrest. If they were not imprisoned, they were to proceed to the coal mines at Newcastle and urge the indentured Indian workers there to go on strike in protest against the three-pound tax.

When Kasturbai heard these plans she asked her husband indignantly, "What is wrong with me?"

Gandhi surveyed her fondly. Although she was now in her early forties, Kasturbai was still attractive. Her hair had begun to gray, and there were fine lines around her eyes, but the red dot on her forehead that indicated her married status marked a smooth, beautiful brow. Due to her husband's insistence on the Simple Life, she wore no jewelry, and her sari was made of coarse cotton.

During the past few years the relationship between Gandhi and his wife had improved greatly. They had become a devoted, smoothly working team. Kasturbai did not understand her husband but she had come to believe that he was a saint and a genius. If it was difficult to live with such an extraordinary man, it was nevertheless a great privilege to be able to serve him. Besides, Kasturbai now appreciated the tremendous progress Gandhi had made in self-control. No longer did he lose patience with her or shout at her.

"Nothing is wrong with you," Gandhi replied now. "You are, as you have ever been, a good wife to me and a devoted mother to our four sons."

"Then why," she demanded, "am I not considered worthy of taking part in your work? Why do you allow other women to march in satyagraha but exclude me?"

Kasturbai's wish to take an active part in the protest movement delighted Gandhi. He sent her, with a second group of women, in the opposite direction from the first group, to go from Natal into the Transvaal. These women were arrested almost at once and thrown into jail.

The women who went in the other direction, to the Newcastle coal mines, were not immediately arrested. They persuaded the miners to go on strike. Then at last the government acted, and these women were imprisoned too.

Other indentured miners went on strike, and the movement spread. It threatened to paralyze all mines and all labor. Gandhi hurried to Newcastle to prevent violence.

The government, trying to force the miners to return to work, shut off electricity and water in their homes, which were owned by the company. Instead of returning to the mines, however, the strikers took their families and left their homes, carrying bundles on their heads. They gathered near the house where Gandhi was now staying. In a few days 2,000 miners were sleeping under the stars and eating what food the Indian merchants of the area contributed. More strikers were arriving daily. In a week the crowd had swelled to 4,000.

Gandhi was in a quandary. Something had to be done, and soon. The strike might last for months. Local merchants could not be expected to feed this growing throng much longer. It was clearly up to him to care for them. What should he do?

Suddenly the answer came to Gandhi through an "inner voice." He would lead this army of miners across the border into the Transvaal, breaking the law against going from one province to another without a permit. The men would all be arrested, and they would have to serve jail terms; while there they would be fed and housed by the government.

Gandhi explained his plan carefully to the miners. He made sure they knew what they were getting into, by picturing life in jail as darkly as possible.

"The easiest course for you," he told them frankly, "would be to return to work. If you cannot face the hardships and the brutality you can expect in jail, without resorting to violence, then return to your homes at once. No one will think the less of you if you turn back now."

Not one striker returned to the mines. All of them promised to follow Gandhi and to obey his orders to the letter.

"Very well, then," said Gandhi. "You will behave decently and morally on the march. You will not touch anyone's property along the way. You will follow my instructions about sanitation in our camps.

"Above all, there must be absolutely no violence. If any European tries to arrest you, or abuse you, do not resist. Do not even lift a hand to ward off a blow."

Each striker was given a pound and a half of bread and an ounce of sugar.

"I will try," Gandhi told the men, "to get more food on the way, but I can promise nothing."

With instructions clearly understood, the march began on October 13, 1913. In disciplined, orderly fashion, the great throng walked in the wake of their leader, the little, unimpressive-looking brown-skinned man who had such remarkable power to draw men to him. Mile after mile they marched, with nothing to eat all day long but a few chunks of bread and a taste of sugar. On the second day they arrived in Charleston, near the Transvaal border. There, to Gandhi's relief, a friend waited with rice and vegetables he had gotten from sympathetic Indians in Charleston.

Gandhi now sent a message to the government, announcing his plans. "If the government abolishes the three-pound tax," he said, "the strikers will return to the mines. Otherwise we will continue on into the Transvaal."

The government did not repeal the three-pound tax. Neither did it make a move to arrest any of the strikers.

Again Gandhi was faced with the original problem: what to do with this great band of helpless, illiterate, and impoverished men who looked to him so trustingly for salvation. All were indentured laborers, most of them Untouchables. There was no one else they could turn to for help.

Years ago Gandhi had decided that all of mankind was his family. Now he was, in very fact, expected to act like a father to several thousand men and a number of women and children.

There was only one solution. If the government would not feed them, he must lead them to Tolstoy Farm, where they could raise their own food and at least subsist until the strike was settled. By marching twenty miles each day for eight days, they would reach Tolstoy. A European baker in the next town volunteered to supply bread for the "army" each day, shipping it by rail to certain stations along the route.

Gandhi arranged a chain of command so the march would not be leaderless if he were arrested. The men were told who would take his place, and who would step into the post of command if that leader were arrested, and so on. Only those strong enough to take the long march would go.

At 6:30 A.M. on November 6, over 2,200 strikers left Charleston. That night, after eating their meager ration of bread and sugar, the miners settled down to sleep on the hard ground. Gandhi prepared to join them. Then he noticed a light bobbing toward him through the big camp. When it came closer, he saw it was a lantern carried by a policeman.

The officer stopped when he reached Gandhi. "I have a warrant for your arrest."

Gandhi woke the man who had been selected as his first replacement and turned over the command to him. Then he accompanied the policemen to jail. In a little while he was released on bail and rejoined the marchers.

The next day Gandhi was arrested again. Once more he was released on bail. Two days later he was jailed for the third time. In four days he had been arrested three times! On his third arrest he was kept in prison and sentenced to three months at hard labor.

Eventually, all leaders of the march were jailed. The strikers themselves were arrested and herded back to the mines by train. They were kept in stockades and treated like cattle. Although they were whipped, kicked, and beaten, and some died, the survivors steadfastly refused to go down into the coal mines.

In sympathy with the Newcastle miners, more and more laborers went on strike. Finally 50,000 jammed the prisons.

Gandhi's weekly paper, *Indian Opinion*, which had managed to continue publication, kept the world informed about the great march. From around the globe came criticism of the South African government.

On December 19, 1913, Gandhi and the other leaders of the movement were released from prison. Three days later Gandhi appeared at a mass meeting in Durban in bare feet, with his mustache shaved off. In place of smart European clothes, which he had worn for more than twenty years, he was now dressed merely in a loincloth and sandals like the poorest peasant. This attire, Gandhi announced, was a sign of mourning for the dead strikers. Indians and Europeans alike understood that Gandhi no longer wanted to look like a European after the way the British and the Boers had treated his people.

A few months later General Smuts sent for Gandhi. They held many talks and exchanged numerous letters. Finally, they reached an agreement. Hindu, Muslim, and Parsi marriages were declared valid, and the three-pound tax on indentured laborers was abolished.

The settlement represented compromise on both sides. To Gandhi the agreement was important because it established the principle of racial equality, and it proved the power of satyagraha.

"Satyagraha is a force," Gandhi wrote in *Indian Opinion*, "which, if it became universal, would revolutionize social ideals and do away with despotism and . . . militarism. . . ."

On July 18, 1914, Gandhi left South Africa forever. He believed that his work there was finished. He thought he had converted General Smuts to "right-doing." Now he would return to India.

The Gandhis—Mohandas and Kasturbai—shortly after their return to India with their family

10.   Champion of the Oppressed

While Gandhi was on his way home, World War I broke out in Europe. However, the war had little effect on his life in India at first.

Gandhi made no attempt to establish a law practice there. He had come to feel that earning money did not fit in with the Simple Life, even if the money was used in social work. Besides, he intended to transplant satyagraha to India, since it had proved to be a successful method of revolt for an unarmed people.

Gandhi's first project was to establish an *ashram*, a colony like Phoenix and Tolstoy Farm. He rented some land near Ahmedabad, a great textile manufacturing city in western India. Some whitewashed mud huts were built, and gardens and orchards started. The women did the laundry in the nearby Sabarmati River, while sacred cows waded around them and over their clean clothes. Besides keeping his own plate, bedroom, and living quarters clean, each resident was expected to do some physical labor for the "family." Each member had to take fourteen vows, including those of truth, nonviolence, non-possession or voluntary poverty, fearlessness, chastity, and anti-Untouchability. Several local millowners contributed to the support of the settlement.

Gandhi's two older sons were not with him now. Harilal had left after a bitter quarrel. Harilal had always resented his lack of education, and he felt that his father did not really love him. Gandhi had sent Manilal back to South Africa to edit *Indian Opinion*, so only the two youngest boys, Ramdas and Devadas, were with their parents. But everyone in the ashram called Gandhi *Bapu*, or father.

Gandhi turned over the management of the settlement to Maganlal Gandhi, a loyal, hard-working cousin who had been with him in South Africa for years. He himself had a tiny room, with a single small window which opened onto a terrace. There he worked and slept the year round, except when he was traveling. On the river bank he held daily prayer meetings. From far and near people from all walks of life came to the meetings. Occasionally one of them applied for admission to the ashram.

One day an Untouchable, Dudabhai, asked to be admitted to the settlement. Gandhi was delighted. To serve notice on the world that he hated Untouchability and intended to stamp it out, he gladly admitted Dudabhai and his wife and child.

At once a storm broke. Orthodox Hindus in the area

protested hotly against Untouchables living in their neighborhood. The man in charge of the local well would not let the ashram residents draw water from it.

"Drops from your buckets would defile me," he insisted. He swore at Dudabhai and abused him. He cursed the entire ashram.

"What shall we do?" Gandhi's followers asked him. "We must have water."

"Continue to draw water," Gandhi replied calmly. "Pay no attention to the man's curses and abuse. Eventually he will leave us alone."

Gandhi was right. The well supervisor finally stopped tormenting them.

Then Gandhi learned that Kasturbai and other Hindu women were discriminating against the Untouchable woman. They refused to allow her to cook in the community kitchen, or to wash clothes in the river. At once Gandhi ordered this treatment to stop.

"You ask more of us than flesh and blood can bear!" Kasturbai protested.

"I ask of you nothing more than I require of myself," he replied, "to treat every other human being as I would like to be treated."

"But you are a saint," Kasturbai wailed. "You can bear things that ordinary mortals cannot."

"With the help of God you can bear anything he requires of you," Gandhi told her sternly. "There will be no more discrimination against Untouchables." His command was obeyed.

One day Maganlal Gandhi, who managed the finances, reported, "We have little money left, Bapu. The men in Ahmedabad who have been supporting our ashram stopped sending money when the Untouchable family came."

"Very well," Gandhi replied tranquilly. "When our money is gone, we will go to live in the Untouchables' ghetto in Ahmedabad. We will earn our living as sweepers or garbage collectors."

The women gasped in horror. They had no doubt that Bapu would do exactly as he said.

The following morning one of the children came running up to Gandhi.

"There is a man outside, Bapu," she cried. "He must be very rich, for he drives a fine car. He wants to see you."

When Gandhi went out to the car, he recognized the occupant as Sheth Ambalal who lived nearby.

"I want to help your ashram," said Ambalal. "Will you accept money from me?"

"Certainly," Gandhi replied.

"I shall return tomorrow at this same hour," said the man, and he drove away.

The next day, at precisely the same time, the big car again drew up in front of the ashram. Again Gandhi went out to greet Ambalal. The caller handed him a bag of money. "I hope this will be enough," he said. He drove away quickly, with Gandhi's amazed thanks ringing in his ears.

When the money had been counted, Maganlal announced joyfully, "It is enough to support our ashram for an entire year, Bapu!"

"Surely," said Gandhi, "God sent Sheth Ambalal."

Indian nationalists who had followed Gandhi's exploits in South Africa had expected great things of him. As the months went by, however, they became disillusioned. Why, he was accomplishing absolutely nothing in India!

Gandhi was not yet ready for action. He must familiarize himself with conditions in India first to see what was needed. He traveled around the country talking to people, from princely rulers to starving peasants and Untouchables. He learned, first hand, what life in India was like. India, he saw, was a land of heat, earthquakes, monsoons, and floods. He saw that farmers sat idle half the year, when the earth was too dry to farm. He learned that the many different languages made communication almost impossible; there were eighteen major languages in India and about 200 more dialects. He discovered that boys who had been taught to read in school forgot how after they returned to their villages, because there were no books there.

If the ignorance of rural India shocked Gandhi, its poverty appalled him. Fully three-fourths of the population suffered from malnutrition. Until their bodies were made strong, little could be done about improving their minds and their spirits. Millions died in famines each year, more millions in epidemics, and 20,000 were killed annually by wild beasts.

By the time he had been in India two years, Gandhi had become acquainted with the leading Indian nationalists. Like them, he wanted self-government for India. Unlike them, he did not advocate complete independence. Instead, he favored dominion status, such as Canada and Australia had.

Many of Gandhi's ideas about India's future were not popular with the intellectuals of the Indian National Congress. They wanted India to be modernized and industrialized, like Europe and the United States. Gandhi, on the other hand, recommended a return to the rural economy with cottage industries that India had had for thousands of years. In living a Simple Life, Gandhi believed, Indians would develop self-discipline and self-reliance. Only then would they be ready for self-rule.

In December, 1916, Gandhi attended the annual convention of the Indian National Congress in Lucknow. There he talked to 26-year-old Jawaharlal Nehru and his father, the wealthy lawyer, Motilal, members of the proud Brahman caste. Fastidious young Jawaharlal was

In the India to which Gandhi returned, farmers lived in crude mud huts and tried to work the baked soil with primitive equipment.

not particularly impressed with Gandhi. The way the little man insisted on mopping toilets at the Congress camps, for instance, was absolutely ridiculous!

Gandhi, however, liked both Nehrus at once. He would keep an eye on young Jawaharlal.

After one of the Congress meetings a skinny peasant waylaid Gandhi.

"I am Rajkumar Shukla, an indigo farmer from Champaran," he said. "I want you to come to my district and help my people."

Most of the land in the Champaran district, at the foot of the Himalayas, Gandhi learned, was divided into huge estates. They were owned by absentee English landlords and worked by Indian tenants. Each peasant was obliged to plant fifteen per cent of his land with indigo, which was used to make dyes. The entire indigo crop must be surrendered to the landlord.

"Some day I will come to your district," Gandhi said, "and check the facts, but now I have to go to another meeting." He listed the cities he had promised to visit, to show that he was not merely making excuses.

The peasant nodded and left. But when Gandhi reached his meeting place there was Shukla waiting.

"Champaran is very near here," he said. "Please come with me for a day."

"I will come some day," Gandhi assured him. "But I have several other appointments first."

When Gandhi returned to his ashram a few weeks later, there was Shukla.

"Now will you come?" he begged. "Tell me when you will come."

Gandhi considered. "I must be in Calcutta several weeks from now. Meet me at this address and I will go with you to Champaran."

When Gandhi reached his destination in Calcutta, the first person he saw was Shukla, squatting patiently in front of the house, waiting.

In April, 1917, when Gandhi had finished his business in Calcutta, the two set out for the indigo plantations.

Gandhi soon learned that the sharecroppers had many grievances besides the fifteen per cent indigo crop that their landlords demanded. Most of these peasants lived in extreme poverty. They did not dare to complain to the overseer of their plantation about anything, or they would be beaten, and their cottages looted and perhaps burned. Now they had discovered that their landlords were cheating them badly.

Germany had recently developed synthetic indigo, and this had ruined the market for natural indigo. The illiterate peasants, isolated from the world, had not learned about synthetic indigo. The wealthy landlords took advantage of this ignorance. Since their indigo plantations were no longer profitable, they wanted the peasants to make up their losses. They offered to release the sharecroppers from their fifteen per cent contracts for a lump sum of money or an outrageous increase in rent.

Most of the peasants paid willingly one way or the other, relieved to be freed from the hated indigo contracts. Others refused to pay, and they were beaten and threatened with death. The landlords had already collected more than 90,000 pounds ($450,000) in outright payments, besides huge rent increases, but still they were not satisfied.

The news about synthetic indigo had reached this isolated district at last, and the peasants realized they had been robbed. They asked for their money back, but the English landlords only laughed at them.

When Gandhi came to Champaran, he intended to stay only a few days. He remained a year.

It did not take him long to decide in his own mind that the landlords were guilty of dishonesty and inhuman treatment. If he was to help the tenants, however, he must collect evidence.

First Gandhi tried to find out the landlords' side of the matter, but no Englishman would talk to him. Instead, Gandhi was ordered to leave the district. He refused, and was summoned to appear in court.

Gandhi knew he would probably go to jail. But the investigation must go on. Before obeying the court summons, he telegraphed a full report to the viceroy. He telegraphed to several Indian lawyers, asking them to come to his aid, and he sent for helpers from his ashram.

Gandhi was not imprisoned after all, and his case was dropped. With the help of the lawyers who answered his appeal, Gandhi recorded the sharecroppers' complaints. Thousands of peasants traveled on foot from every corner of the province to see him. Although they were afraid to tell their grievances to their landlords, they spoke freely to Gandhi. None had ever heard of him before or of his work in South Africa, but they trusted him on sight. He dressed as simply as they did, and he seemed to understand their thoughts. They told others about him.

Soon Gandhi found it difficult to move from place to place. Adoring crowds followed him, begging for *darshan*, which is spiritual tonic or blessing. To the peasants, Gandhi was a holy man, and all Indians revere and cherish holy men.

During the months Gandhi remained in Champaran, he did many things for the peasants. His wife Kasturbai, his youngest son Devadas, and several others had come from the ashram at his request. With their help and that of volunteers from other provinces, Gandhi started schools for the sharecroppers' children. He also obtained doctors' services, and he taught the peasants about sanitation. One volunteer teacher, Mahadev Desai, was so devoted that he became Gandhi's permanent secretary.

At last, the government appointed an official commission to investigate the tenants' situation. Gandhi was the peasants' representative.

When the landlords saw the huge stack of documents and signed statements that had been collected, they promised to refund part of the money to their tenants. Gandhi finally agreed to settle for twenty-five per cent.

"It isn't the amount of the payment that is important," he said. "It's the principle that these peasants have rights. The landlords will not again try to grind them down under their heels."

Gandhi was right. In a few years the British landlords abandoned their unprofitable estates, and the tenants became owners of the land.

To the Indians, who had been ordered around by the English all their lives, Gandhi's accomplishment in Champaran was a triumph for the entire Indian people, a breath of hope for the future.

11. The Peaceful Fighter in India

Gandhi wanted to stay longer in Champaran, but he was called home because of unrest in the textile mills in Ahmedabad.

When Gandhi reached Ahmedabad, he talked to many mill hands. "We are overworked and underpaid," they insisted. "We want more money and better working conditions."

Gandhi visited the mills and the homes of the employees. Living conditions were dreadful. Often, a dozen people lived in a single room. Some people had no homes at all, and slept on the pavement. In many huge apartment houses, the middle rooms had practically no ventilation. Toilet facilities were primitive and totally inadequate. Household filth and garbage were dumped outside.

The mill hands usually had to work twelve hours a day, with few and inadequate safety devices. Wages were miserably small. Most of the workers were always in debt.

Gandhi approached the mill owners about wage increases and factory improvements, but they only laughed.

The leader of the mill owners said to Gandhi, "You know nothing about the situation. Our workers are our children, and no outsider can tell us how to take care of them."

Gandhi urged the mill owners to submit the dispute to arbitration. "Let each side choose a representative, and both sides agree on an impartial third party. Let this arbitration board rule on the case."

The employers refused flatly. So Gandhi called a meeting of the labor leaders. He advised them to go on strike. He helped them organize the strike, and he himself laid down the rules.

A mass meeting of the strikers was held on the bank of the Sabarmati River. Gandhi, standing under a huge banyan tree, addressed the meeting.

"This is to be no ordinary strike," he told the workers. "There must be no violence whatever. If your employers bring in strikebreakers, you must not bother them. You should all find some other work, some honest source of income, to live on while the strike lasts."

The laborers accepted the rules Gandhi laid down. They stood up, 10,000 strong, and repeated after him a solemn pledge:

"We will not return to our jobs until our terms are

met, or our employers agree to refer the dispute to arbitration."

Every afternoon at 4:30 the strikers met on the bank of the river. Thousands attended the meetings. The men sang and shouted slogans. Their favorite was one which Gandhi had given them:

"Be not afraid, for we have a divine helper." Gandhi, of course, meant that God was their helper, but to most of the workers the divine one was Gandhi himself.

Gandhi attended every meeting. Each day he made a speech, encouraging the men and reminding them to avoid violence. Each day at the close of the meeting, the strikers stood and repeated their pledge in unison. Then they paraded through the streets of the city in orderly fashion, carrying banners that read, "Keep the Pledge."

One week went by, then another. Several times Gandhi approached the mill owners and urged them to arbitrate, but always they refused. Some of them employed strikebreakers and continued to operate their mills as before.

Gradually the determination of the strikers began to weaken. Fewer and fewer attended the daily meetings. Each time Gandhi asked them to repeat their pledge, their voices sounded less resolute. He feared they would soon break and return to their jobs in spite of their promise. Few had been able to find other work.

On the eighteenth afternoon of the strike, when Gandhi attended the daily meeting on the river bank, he was greatly troubled. As he stood under the banyan tree to make his usual talk, he looked into hundreds of unhappy, uncertain faces. What could he say, he wondered, to strengthen them, and to persuade them to remain true to their pledge?

Suddenly Gandhi recalled a striker's remark that had been repeated to him: "It is nothing to the leaders that we suffer. They have plenty of food, but we are starving."

Gandhi found himself saying to the crowd, "Until the strike is settled, or the dispute referred to arbitration, I will not touch any food whatever."

The mill hands stared at him, shocked by his words. Protests began to rise from all sides.

"Not you, Bapu!"

"We should fast, but not you!"

"Do not fast, Bapu! We will be faithful to our pledge."

But Gandhi stood firm. A vow was a vow. "My fast will be broken only when the strike is settled." Ashamed and worried, the mill hands dispersed.

When the leader of the employers learned about the fast, he hurried to the ashram and accused Gandhi of putting unfair pressure on the mill owners.

"I had no intention of putting pressure on you,"

Gandhi replied. "Since I represent the laborers, I must take on myself the guilt for their failings."

"It's easy for you to talk like that!" the mill owner snapped. "You know perfectly well that we cannot stand by and see you ruin your health and perhaps die. We do not want your blood on our hands."

Three days later the 21-day strike was settled. Kasturbai brought her husband a glass of orange juice and the fast ended.

The following month Gandhi led a successful satyagraha campaign in another district for peasants who were being unfairly taxed. Indian leaders and British officials alike began to realize that Gandhi was a man to reckon with.

World War I was now in its fourth year. England needed more soldiers, and the government persuaded Gandhi to undertake a recruiting campaign. Gandhi agreed because he still felt that citizens of the Empire should help when help was needed. Besides, he was given to understand that India's assistance would be rewarded with self-government when war ended.

In Gandhi's previous travels around India, he had been welcomed as a holy man. Assistance had been freely offered. He had never had to pay for food or lodging or a bullock cart. But now that he represented the British government, trying to enlist soldiers for the hated British army, he was received coldly. No one volunteered a bit of help. He could not even hire a bullock cart. He often walked 20 miles a day, carrying his own food, which at that time was mostly lemons and peanut butter. He slept out in the open without bedding.

The recruiting campaign nearly wrecked Gandhi's health. He fell desperately ill. Doctors and hospitals could do nothing for him, because he stubbornly refused all medicines, all injections, and all foods except fruit, vegetables, and cereals. No meat, no eggs, no milk —nothing that the doctors prescribed to build up his strength would Gandhi accept. He grew weaker and weaker, and thinner and thinner. Finally, he insisted on being carried to his ashram to die.

He summoned his followers to his bedside. "My last message to India," he said, "is that she will find her salvation through nonviolence."

Each person present believed he had heard Bapu's dying words. Tears flowed freely.

But Kasturbai would not give up. She called in another doctor. He too advised milk. Weak as he was, Gandhi flatly refused it. "I took a vow against milk," he said stubbornly.

Kasturbai, standing beside her husband's pallet, spoke up tartly. "You took a vow against cow's milk and buffalo milk, but there was nothing whatever in your vow about goat's milk."

The doctor applauded the suggestion, and some goat's milk was brought. Gandhi allowed himself to be persuaded to drink it, and goat's milk became part of his regular diet. Little by little he regained his strength.

Years later Gandhi admitted that drinking goat's milk broke the spirit of his vow, if not the letter. "The will to live was stronger," he said, "than the love of truth."

World War I ended on November 11, 1918, but India was not given self-government. Instead, she was oppressed more than ever.

Throughout the war England had imposed on India laws that curtailed freedom of speech and of the press. Newspapers were censored, and people who criticized government policies were imprisoned without trial. These laws infuriated Indians, but everyone believed that they would be repealed when the war ended. On the contrary, the so-called Rowlatt Bills, which made these laws permanent, were passed on March 18, 1919.

To Gandhi, as to other Indian nationalist leaders, the Rowlatt Bills were unbearable. He tried to think of some way to launch a satyagraha campaign against them.

One night Gandhi had a dream in which he saw a plan of action. The next morning he announced, "We will call on the entire country to observe a general *hartal*. This will serve notice on the British that all India is united in opposition to the Rowlatt Bills."

A hartal is a day of fasting and prayer, customary in

India for religious observances. On such a day all businesses close, and no work of any kind is done.

"It is fitting," Gandhi said, "that we begin our satyagraha campaign with a hartal, for ours is a holy fight."

Other leaders agreed to his plan, and a hartal was announced for the entire country, to be held on March 30, 1919. Later the date was changed to April 6. Still weak from his recent illness, Gandhi toured the land to educate the people in satyagraha. Then he traveled to the city of Bombay to observe the hartal.

On the morning of April 6, thousands of Bombay citizens, including a number of women and children, marched to the sea to bathe. Prayers in temples and mosques followed, then processions and speeches.

Gandhi explained the plans for satyagraha, and he read a pledge of resistance to the Rowlatt Bills.

> Until they are withdrawn we shall refuse civilly to obey these laws and such other laws as a committee . . . may think fit, and we further affirm that in this struggle we shall faithfully follow truth and refrain from violence to life, person, and property.

All day long not a wheel turned in Bombay. Not a shop, or an office, or a classroom opened. Not a ship was loaded or unloaded. Not a vehicle was for hire. In the entire great city, only the English tried to work, and they were utterly helpless without their Indian assistants.

Gandhi was pleased with the success of the hartal in Bombay and the start of his satyagraha campaign.

Then reports began to trickle in from other places, and the picture changed drastically. There had been violence in Delhi, India's capital, and even in Ahmedabad. In the city of Amritsar, in the Punjab province, a frightful massacre had taken place. Gandhi's close friend, Charles F. Andrews, a dedicated Christian missionary who had worked in India many years, sent him the horrible details.

Amritsar's hartal had passed peacefully enough; Europeans walked through the streets untouched. But the government arrested two Indian leaders and banished them from the province. A mob gathered, violence broke out, and there was no leader to stop it. Several British businessmen were killed, and a woman schoolteacher, Miss Sherwood, was brutally slain.

Brigadier General Dyer came to Amritsar with an army. He read a proclamation, in English, prohibiting meetings of any kind. Few Indian citizens heard it, or understood it if they did.

At 4 P.M. on April 13, about 20,000 Indians gathered in a great walled courtyard for a previously planned meeting. The British general led his mounted troops inside the courtyard. For ten minutes the soldiers fired into the helpless penned-in throng. Hundreds were killed, and thousands wounded.

Not satisfied with this brutality, General Dyer machine-gunned a number of villages. In addition, he forced all Indians to get out of cars and buses and salute each passing European. He made college students march sixteen miles a day in the sweltering heat to respond to roll call.

Worst of all was Dyer's infamous "crawling order."

"Any Indian," the general announced, "who passes, for any reason whatever, the street where Miss Sherwood was attacked, must crawl on all fours."

The officers who carried out this order forced the Indians to wriggle along the street like snakes.

This "crawling order" struck at the Indians' cherished dignity. More than anything that had been done in 150 years of oppression, it turned Indians against their English rulers.

It turned Gandhi against them, too. Still, he could not allow his indignation at General Dyer's inhumanity to affect his conduct of the satyagraha campaign. Since there had been violence on the part of his own people, satyagraha—dedicated to nonviolence—had failed. He called off the campaign abruptly, and undertook a three-day fast to atone for the failings of his followers.

"I have made a Himalayan miscalculation," he said, "in believing that my people were ready for satyagraha. I underrated the forces of evil."

Indians all over the country were confused by Gandhi's sudden turnabout. First he had urged them to offer civil disobedience to British laws. Now he told them to cooperate with their oppressors. What were they to think?

Gandhi had recently assumed the editorship of two weekly papers, *Young India,* printed in English, and *Navajivan,* an Indian language paper. In these newspapers he wrote many articles about satyagraha. By the time the next struggle started, he hoped that the people would understand it and would refrain from violence.

12. Spinner in a Loincloth

Gandhi believed he had found a way to get self-rule for India—he would revive hand-spinning.

One of Britain's chief interests in India had always been the cotton that Indian farmers raised. The cotton was shipped to England, spun and woven in British factories, and then the cloth was shipped back to India to be sold. The cottage industry of hand-spinning, so widespread a century earlier among Indian peasants, had died out. If hand-spinning was revived, Indians could spin and weave their own cloth instead of buying English goods. Then there would be no market in India for the British product. Gandhi believed that the British Empire would soon lose interest in a country that brought it no wealth, and would gladly grant it self-rule.

Gandhi himself learned to spin, and after that he spent half an hour a day at his spinning wheel. The members of the ashram also learned to spin and weave, and soon all were wearing *khadi*, or coarse homespun clothing. The custom spread, and Nationalist leaders wore khadi too.

In December, 1920, the Indian National Congress met at Nagpur. Gandhi had drafted a new constitution for the Congress, which changed it from a debating society of upper-caste Indians to an effective democratic organization. There were units for each village, each city, each province. For the first time the Congress became important in the lives of India's millions.

At the Nagpur meeting, the Congress passed the following resolutions proposed by Gandhi:

> The goal of the Congress was to be self-rule, within the British Empire if possible, or outside if necessary.
>
> Untouchability was to be removed from India.
>
> Hand-spinning and hand-weaving were to be revived throughout the country.
>
> Noncooperation with the British government would begin immediately. There would be four stages; the final one would involve nonpayment of taxes.

"The only true resistance to the British government," Gandhi told the Congress, "is to stop cooperating with it. Let us all give up our jobs in government, whether in civil service, or in law courts, or in any field whatever. Let us take our children out of English schools and colleges. Let us return all titles and honors that the British government has given us. Let us boycott English goods. By ceasing all forms of cooperation with the English government, we will serve immediate notice that we want a government of our own, as we were promised during the war."

Many influential Indians renounced their titles and returned their decorations. Wealthy Motilal Nehru gave up his law practice and his luxurious western-styled home, and began to live like a simple Indian peasant. He became a total noncooperator. His brilliant son Jawaharlal, and many other successful lawyers, also left the English courts and became noncooperators. Jawaharlal now was one of Gandhi's admirers.

To get the support of the masses for his noncooperation campaign, Gandhi set out on a seven-month tour of the country. There was no radio network at that time to broadcast his words to the far provinces, and few of India's millions could read his weekly papers, even if they saw them. Going to the people was the quickest way of explaining noncooperation.

Gandhi traveled mostly by train, using third-class compartments. They were hot, dirty, smelly, and incredibly crowded. He had little appetite for the food he carried, usually bread, oranges, and some raisins.

At each train stop Gandhi addressed great mass meetings. Sometimes 100,000 people would gather to hear him. Mostly they were drawn, not by the desire to learn about noncooperation, but by the wish to receive his darshan. People believed that the blessing of the Mahatma, the Great Soul, as many now called him, could cure all ills. Thousands fell on their knees before him. People fought to kiss his feet. To Gandhi this adoration was a great trial, yet he understood the need of his people for a religious leader.

At each meeting Gandhi explained the meaning of noncooperation in simple terms. He stressed the importance of hand-spinning.

"Do you want self-rule for India?" he would ask. A wild cheer would answer him. "Then give up your English clothes. Take off, here and now, everything you are wearing that is foreign-made. Let us make a bonfire of these textiles that keep India in subjection to British masters."

The response was immediate and practically universal. Some men stripped off *all* their clothes! Coats, hats, shirts, trousers, shoes, socks, underwear—all were passed from hand to hand to the platform and thrown in a great heap in front of it. Then Gandhi struck a match and set fire to the pile. He himself wore nothing but a homespun loincloth, unless the weather called for a shawl. He fastened a cheap, heavy, old-

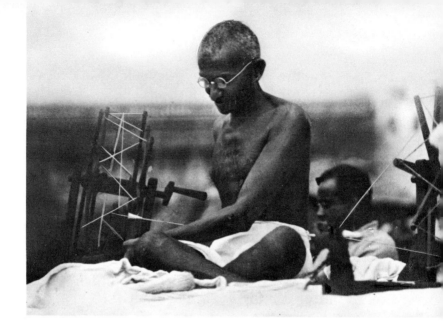

fashioned watch to his loincloth with a safety pin, so that he could keep track of his appointments.

As the flames leaped and crackled, he would resume his speech. "Do not think to replace this clothing with garments fashioned from cloth made in our own mills and factories," he warned. "You must learn to spin and weave. Not until the spinning wheel finds a place of honor in every home in India will we be ready for home rule. Let the spinning wheel be our national symbol of political freedom. Spinning is a means of self-reliance, self-respect, and ultimately to self-government."

He had recently designed a new flag for India, a tricolor of saffron, white, and green, with a spinning wheel in the center.

Gandhi, left, set an example for Indians by spinning a little every day. Congress members, right, check on the sale of cloth made in England and, below, carry a poster announcing the amount of homespun which has been produced.

December of 1921 found Gandhi back home in his ashram. Noncooperation was now in full swing all over India. Thousands were serving terms in jail; among these were the Nehrus, father and son.

To Gandhi's sorrow, however, noncooperation was not always nonviolent. Riots broke out in Bombay, and 58 persons were killed. Gandhi, deeply hurt by this lapse from discipline, fasted five days in penance for his followers. A few months later further riots followed in Chauri Chaura, a tiny village in a remote corner of India. More people were killed. Gandhi called a complete halt to the noncooperation campaign.

This brought a storm of protest. Jawaharlal Nehru, still in prison, demanded, "What does it matter if there has been violence in an unknown village? The non-cooperation movement has passed through one phase after another, and in some places people are clamoring to start the final phase, nonpayment of taxes. Why stop the campaign now?"

Gandhi wrote back, "I had received complaints from many places that noncooperation had been getting out of hand. The Chauri Chaura riot was the last straw. I assure you that if the campaign had not been called off we would have been leading, not a nonviolent struggle, but essentially a violent one."

Again India had failed to follow satyagraha. Again Gandhi fasted five days in penance for his people.

13. The Great Trial

All during the noncooperation campaign the viceroy had hesitated to take action against Gandhi for fear the people would riot. Now that the movement had been cut short, he felt free to act.

At 10:30 P.M. on March 10, 1922, a policeman came to Gandhi's hut in the ashram.

"Are you Mohandas K. Gandhi?" he asked.

From his cross-legged position on the floor, the little brown man in the loincloth looked up at the uniformed English officer. At once he knew why the man had come, and a smile danced in his black eyes.

"Yes, I am."

"I have a warrant for your arrest," the policeman said.

"What is the charge?" Gandhi asked.

"You are charged with exciting disaffection toward His Majesty's Government in India."

"In what way?"

"By publishing seditious articles in your newspapers," the officer replied.

"Will you give me time to clean my teeth?" Gandhi asked. "Also I would like to say good-bye to my family and friends."

The officer agreed, and Gandhi began the fifteen minute ritual of brushing his teeth. Then he called in his family and his followers and told them what had happened. No one made any protest. He had long ago prepared them for his arrest.

Surrounded by his wife, his two youngest sons, and his disciples, Gandhi began to pray aloud. When he finished, he led the group in singing a hymn. One of his favorites was the Christian hymn, "Lead, Kindly Light."

At last Gandhi turned to the impatient policeman and said, "I am ready." With a cheerful smile and a gay wave to those who loved him, 53-year-old Gandhi went off jauntily to jail. He took two blankets, a spare loincloth, and a few books.

On Saturday, March 18, 1922, Gandhi and the printer of *Young India* came to trial in Ahmedabad. The courtroom was jammed with Gandhi's friends.

The offending articles were read to the court, and the charges of "exciting disaffection toward His Majesty's Government" repeated.

"How do you plead?" the judge asked.

"I plead guilty to the charges," Gandhi replied. His voice was steady, but soft and unimpressive as usual.

The prosecutor proceeded to state his case. He accused Gandhi of being a lifelong rebel and agitator.

At last the judge asked, "Mr. Gandhi, do you wish to make a statement?"

"Yes, your honor," Gandhi replied. "I would like to read a statement I have prepared."

Before beginning to read, Gandhi admitted that the prosecutor's accusations were all justified. Then he read his statement. It reviewed his public life, both in South Africa and in India, and then continued:

> I came reluctantly to the conclusion that British rule has made India more helpless than she ever was before. . . . The law in this country has been used to serve the foreign exploiter. . . . In ninety-nine cases out of a hundred, justice has been denied to Indians as against Europeans. . . .
>
> In my humble opinion, *noncooperation with evil is as much a duty as is cooperation with good*. . . . I am here, therefore, to . . . submit cheerfully to the highest penalty that can be inflicted on me. . . .

The judge sentenced Gandhi to six years' imprisonment and the printer to one year.

When court adjourned most of the spectators fell at Gandhi's feet and wept. The leave-taking took almost an hour. Officers, who were waiting to escort him to prison, stood silently by until he was ready to join them.

Gandhi's merciless criticism of British rule made headlines around the world. The trial became known as "The Great Trial." An Indian poet compared it to the trial of Jesus.

In spite of prison restrictions, Gandhi was not unhappy. At first books were forbidden, and also his spinning wheel, but in a few weeks both bans were lifted. After that he kept his regular routine, with daily walks, spinning, and morning and evening prayers. He received little news from the outside world, because newspapers were forbidden. He was allowed only one carefully screened visitor each month, and once a month he could send a censored letter to his family or friends.

While Gandhi was in jail he wrote the *History of Satyagraha in South Africa*, detailing his twenty years of work in Africa. He also started his autobiography, which he called, *The Story of My Experiments with Truth.*

In January, 1924, when Gandhi had been in prison nearly two years, he had an acute attack of appendicitis. An immediate operation was advised.

After his release from prison, Gandhi wrote letters and rested in this seashore cottage near Bombay.

The British prison and hospital officials were greatly worried. They had heard of Gandhi's stubborn refusal of medication during his near-fatal illness of 1918, after the recruiting campaign. If he should refuse to be operated on now, and should die on their hands, all of India might rise against them. There was no telling to what lengths the masses might go if the Mahatma, their beloved holy man, were allowed to die.

To the immense relief of the prison authorities, Gandhi consented to the operation. In spite of a terrific thunderstorm which cut off the hospital's electricity, the operation was a success.

But Gandhi did not get well as fast as the doctors expected, so on February 5, 1924, the government released him from prison.

14. The Salt March

As soon as he regained his health, Gandhi resumed the editorship of *Young India* and *Navajivan,* which his secretary, Mahadev, had carried on during his two-year imprisonment.

Gandhi soon realized that while he had been in jail the political situation in India had changed. Hindus and Muslims were at each other's throats. The Muslim slaughter of cows infuriated Hindus, while the Muslims took as deadly insults the Hindu noise and music during their twice-daily prayer times. Each group resented the political influence and the wealth of the other. Recently the Muslims, under the leadership of Mohammed Ali Jinnah, had left the Indian National Congress and had formed the Muslim League.

Through the pages of his weekly papers, Gandhi tried to bring about harmony between Hindus and Muslims, but he could not. Bitter fighting broke out. A riot in Kohat resulted in 155 Hindus being killed and the rest of the Hindu populace being driven out of town. Gandhi felt personally responsible. for this violence. He himself had awakened India to a national consciousness through his noncooperation movement, and now that movement had gotten out of control.

Gandhi came to a grave decision. He announced sadly on September 18, 1924:

> Nothing evidently which I say or write can bring the two communities [Hindus and Muslims] together. Therefore I am imposing on myself a 21-day fast from today, and ending on Wednesday, October 6. I reserve the liberty of drinking water with or without salt. My fast is both a penance and a prayer.... I respectfully invite the heads of all communities, including Englishmen, to meet and end the quarrel which is a disgrace to religion and to humanity. It seems as if God has been dethroned. Let us reinstate Him in our hearts.

Gandhi fasted in the home of a Muslim friend who —like himself—was a champion of Hindu-Muslim friendship. Two Muslim doctors were in constant attendance. Gandhi's loyal friend, Charles Andrews, the Christian missionary, acted as his nurse, and also edited *Young India*.

Gandhi was 55 years old, and he had never been strong. A 21-day fast might kill him. A clamor for action rose from every city and every village of India.

Within a week a "Unity Conference" met at Delhi, with 300 in attendance. Resolutions designed to promote good will between the rival groups were passed, and the conference broke up in an atmosphere of friendship. Hindus and Muslims ate and drank together—something unheard of—and let the world know they were friends. But Gandhi had vowed to fast for 21 days, so he continued.

At first he kept to his daily routine. As the days passed, however, increasing weakness forced him to give up walking, then spinning, then writing, and finally reading. On the twentieth day he was too weak to sit up.

That evening Gandhi lay on his pallet on the open roof of the house. Dozens of his followers came to see him. In the moonlight he looked so frail that their hearts ached. But he was bright and cheerful, although his voice was very weak.

On the last day of the announced fast, at 4 A.M.—Gandhi's customary rising hour—the household assembled by his bed for morning prayers. The moon had long since set, and it was dark and cold.

"How did you sleep, Bapu?" Andrews asked, tenderly tucking the shawl around the thin shoulders.

"Very well indeed," Gandhi replied, smiling cheerfully. To Andrews' relief, the voice was stronger than it had been the previous day.

After prayers a steady stream of people filed past Gandhi's cot for darshan. Many people believed that the mere sight of the Mahatma gave them a blessing.

At midday the entire household gathered around Gandhi, including all the servants and a number of his close friends. Everyone, Hindus and Muslims, sat on the floor.

Before breaking his fast, Gandhi insisted on a ceremony expressing religious unity. The opening verses of the *Koran* were read, a Christian hymn was sung, and verses of a Hindu religious poem were recited.

At last Gandhi spoke. His voice was scarcely more than a whisper. Everyone strained forward to catch the words.

"I ask you," he faltered, "to lay down your lives, if need be, for the cause of brotherhood."

"We will, Mahatma," they promised, "we will indeed."

Another hymn was sung. Then a doctor brought a bowl of orange juice and held it to Gandhi's lips. He took a sip, then another, and another. The long, long fast had ended.

Because of his appendicitis operation, Gandhi had served only a third of his six-year prison sentence. He considered himself, therefore, to be in the custody of the government for the next four years. So he took no active part in politics but devoted himself to the education of the masses.

Although his health was not good, he traveled again from one corner of India to another, trying to reach everyone he had not yet visited. He traveled by train, by bullock cart, and on foot. No village was too small for his attention. At these rural meetings he used his fingers to emphasize the points of his program for India.

"This," he would say, pointing to a finger on his left hand, "is equality for Untouchables. This," pointing to another finger, "is for spinning. This is for avoiding drink and drugs. This is Hindu-Muslim friendship. This is equality for women. And the wrist is nonviolence."

Gandhi also urged the people to abandon the custom of child marriage. He gave them lessons in nutrition, in sanitation, and in nursing. But more than any other point, he stressed spinning.

"For approximately half of the year," he reminded the peasants, "you have no farm work, nothing to do. Instead of remaining idle for so many months, take up spinning. You can spin and weave in your own huts, while your food cooks. True, spinning will not make you rich, but five or six extra rupees a month will enable you to provide two meals a day for your families, instead of a single meal they customarily get. Besides, each hour you spin brings independence for India that much closer."

But independence did not seem to be coming closer. The British made no move to grant India self-rule.

In December of 1928, the Indian National Congress lost patience. A resolution was passed asking the government for dominion status, or self-rule within the Empire, before the end of the following year. If this were not done, India would demand complete independence and would fight for it with nonviolent noncooperation. Gandhi would lead this struggle.

The months passed, and the British Empire did nothing. At midnight on December 31, 1929, the government's year of grace expired. Congress instructed Gandhi to proceed with his anti-government campaign.

Gandhi waited until his inner voice spoke and told him what to do. Then he announced he would begin his civil disobedience movement by breaking the Salt Act.

In India the manufacture of salt was a government monopoly. It was a crime to possess salt that had not been made by the government.

Jawaharlal Nehru, now president of the Congress, criticized Gandhi sharply. "What will that accomplish,

Bapu?" he asked. "Why choose such a cheap, simple product as salt with which to start a nationwide civil disobedience campaign?"

"Salt is the one thing everyone must eat," Gandhi replied. "The peasant needs more than the rich man, because he works in the hot sun day after day."

In his newspapers Gandhi announced, "I will lead a march from my ashram to Dandi, on the seashore. There we will make salt illegally from sea water."

News of Gandhi's plan spread around the world. He received many telegrams of praise and encouragement from America, Europe, and Asia. Reporters were sent from great newspapers to cover the event. Many came prepared to laugh at Gandhi, but they stayed to love and admire him. He welcomed them to the ashram, which now had 230 members.

At 4 A.M. on March 12, 1930, the residents of the ashram rose, said their prayers, and ate breakfast. Then Gandhi, carrying a long bamboo staff, led the way to the road. He was followed by 78 men and women from the ashram; some had trouble keeping the pace set by the 61-year-old leader. Reporters brought up the rear.

Every foot of the winding road was lined with people. Thousands had been standing for hours to see the Mahatma. They knelt at the roadside as Gandhi passed, and many tried to kiss his feet.

With Gandhi leading, the great salt march begins.

"Gandhi! Mahatma!" they shouted. "Victory to Gandhi!"

Gandhi smiled. He waved and kept on marching.

At each village the marchers halted, and Gandhi spoke to the people. He promised to give them a signal when it was time to break the salt laws.

The pilgrims covered about twelve miles a day. People from various villages joined the march, including many women. By the time the sea was reached, on April 5, after 24 days of marching, the original band had swelled to several thousand.

When they arrived in Dandi, the marchers prayed all night long. Before daylight Gandhi named the leaders who would take charge if he himself was arrested.

Then he led his followers to the sea. Just before stepping into the water, he stooped and picked up a pinch of salt from the shore. He held it high in the air.

"Hail, deliverer!" cried a follower joyfully. "Mahatma Gandhi, great and beloved lawbreaker!"

The crowd cheered. "Mahatma Gandhi!" they shouted. "Victory to Gandhi!"

To the newspaper reporters who followed him Gandhi said, "Anyone who is willing to pay the penalty for breaking the salt laws should make salt wherever he wishes."

Now that the signal had been given, the whole country acted. Every villager along India's long seacoast began to make salt. From one side of India to the other people broke the salt laws.

Jawaharlal Nehru admitted that he had been completely wrong. Nothing could have been more dramatic and more effective than the Mahatma's 200-mile march to the sea for a few grains of contraband salt.

The police began to make arrests. Ramdas, Gandhi's third son, was arrested, together with a large group of people from the ashram. However, more and more marchers took their places immediately—there seemed to be no end to the number of resisters.

Early in the morning on May 5, Gandhi was arrested at his camp near Dandi. Again the ritual began:

"Are you Mohandas K. Gandhi?"

"Yes. Have you come to arrest me?"

"Yes."

"Would you mind waiting while I brush my teeth?"

When Gandhi was ready, his followers recited a hymn together. Then they bowed down before the Mahatma and some touched his feet reverently.

"Good-bye," Gandhi said cheerfully. "You know what to do. Continue the fight until the salt tax is repealed."

Calmly he accompanied the officers to their truck. A few hours later he was in jail once more, imprisoned without a trial; the British did not dare to risk a repetition of the "Great Trial."

Although Gandhi's salt marchers remained nonviolent,
they were harassed and beaten by the police.

15. "The Epic Fast"

Gandhi's arrest did not halt the civil disobedience. On the contrary, it spurred people on. The government filled the jails; nearly 100,000 were imprisoned.

With each passing day of civil disobedience, the brutality of the police increased. Newspaper reporters told of watching police crack skulls with gun butts and steel rods, and of seeing armed officers kick unresisting men in the stomach. None of the lawbreakers even raised a hand to ward off a blow. Remembering that Gandhi had canceled the last resistance campaign because of riots, the resisters carefully refrained from violence.

The viceroy, Lord Irwin, wrote to King George V about these newspaper stories: "Your Majesty can hardly fail to have read with amusement the accounts of the several battles. . . ." This unfeeling comment was reported in a thousand newspapers.

The viceroy may have found police brutality amusing, but the rest of the world did not. The British Empire lost much of its prestige, and the English people became aware for the first time how cruelly their country had subjugated India. Most of them were ashamed.

Soon the British government held a Round Table Conference in London to consider the situation in India. Not one representative of the Indian National Congress was invited, and little was accomplished.

Lord Irwin released Gandhi, the Nehrus, and other Congress leaders from prison on January 26, 1931. Motilal Nehru died soon after this, and the whole country mourned.

The viceroy invited Gandhi to his palace for talks. Eventually they reached a compromise agreement, called the Irwin-Gandhi Pact. The viceroy promised that political prisoners would be released, salt manufacturing would be permitted on the coast, and Congress would be invited to send delegates to the Second Round Table Conference.

In return Gandhi called off the civil disobedience movement. To Gandhi this pact was important because the government had negotiated with Indians instead of dictating to them.

Gandhi was unanimously elected by the Congress as its sole delegate to the Second Round Table Conference. His youngest son Devadas accompanied him, and so did his faithful secretary Mahadev. Also in the Gandhi party was a little goat, to provide the daily milk the Mahatma had come to depend on.

Gandhi, wearing loincloth and sandals and carrying a few meager possessions, arrives in London for the Second Round Table Conference.

Gandhi refused many invitations to stay in fine houses or hotels near St. James's Palace where the Round Table Conference was held. Instead, he stayed in an East End Settlement House. Although he attended the conference meetings faithfully, he spent much time getting acquainted with the people of the London slums and learning about their problems. Every day he could be seen surrounded by slum children, laughing, talking, and joking with them, perhaps playing blind man's buff.

One day the Mahatma visited the cotton mills of Lancashire. India's boycott of English goods had hit these factories hard.

Gandhi listened attentively as the factory hands told him how difficult it was to support their families on welfare payments, and how they hated being idle.

Then Gandhi told them the Indian situation. "You have 3,000,000 unemployed here in England," he said. "In India we have nearly 300,000,000 who are unemployed half the year. Your average unemployment monthly payment is 70 shillings. Our average income is seven shillings sixpence a month."

When the textile workers realized the reasons for the boycott of English goods, they forgave him.

During his 84 days in England, Gandhi met many of England's great men. General Smuts, his old adversary from South Africa now in London, invited him for a friendly visit. One of Gandhi's amazing qualities was his ability to keep the friendship and respect of even his most bitter opponents. Smuts said later that Gandhi was one of the great men of the world.

One day Gandhi was invited to Buckingham Palace to have tea with King George V and Queen Mary. He went to the Palace dressed in loincloth, sandals, shawl, and his dollar watch. He wore his eyeglasses, but not his false teeth.

As Gandhi left the Palace afterwards, a reporter asked him, "Do you really think you had enough on?"

Gandhi's eyes twinkled. "The King had enough on for both of us," he replied.

Another reporter asked Gandhi what he called his style of clothes.

"Well," replied Gandhi with his infectious smile, "for golf you Englishmen wear trousers that you call plus fours. Mine are minus fours."

Although nearly everyone in England was friendly and most gracious to Gandhi personally, he accomplished nothing at the Round Table Conference. British leaders seemed determined to hold fast to their control of India. They worked, not to unite her, but to divide her. When Gandhi sailed for home, he was convinced that England would never surrender India voluntarily.

On his arrival in Bombay on December 28, 1931,

Gandhi learned what the British government was doing to keep India powerless. In order to break the growing strength of the Indian National Congress, the government had taken over its funds and disbanded its political organizations. Both of Gandhi's newspapers were suppressed. Jawaharlal Nehru and a Muslim leader had been arrested as they traveled to Bombay to meet him.

Six days later, on January 4, 1932, Gandhi himself was arrested again, along with 15,000 others. By the end of February, 32,600 political prisoners were in jail, without trial, and without bail.

After Gandhi had been in prison for a few months, he learned that the government had proposed a new constitution for India. It would divide Indians into three groups, Hindus, Muslims, and Untouchables. Each group would have its own electorate and vote for its own candidates.

This proposal appalled Gandhi. For years he had worked to make India accept Untouchables into the great family of Indians. He had even adopted as his own the daughter of an Untouchable man who had joined his ashram. Now came the government's proposal for a separate electorate for Untouchables. This plan would guarantee their sharing in the political life of the country, but it would be socially degrading. It would set Untouchables apart permanently.

The government was willing to accept any voting arrangement that Hindus and Untouchables agreed on, but the two groups could not decide. In August the government declared for separate electorates.

Then Gandhi announced, "I must fast unto death against this measure." At 11:30 on the morning of September 20, 1932, he took his last meal, lemon juice and honey, with hot water.

From that hour all of India hung on the news from Gandhi's cell in Yeravda jail. Throughout the length and breadth of the great land rich and poor, high and low, shared a consuming worry about their Mahatma. At frequent intervals news bulletins were broadcast to every part of India. Villages that had no radio got the news by messenger from those that did. People who could not read listened to the newspapers read aloud by others. Everywhere, everywhere one thought dominated India's millions:

"The Mahatma must not die!"

Each Hindu felt that he was personally responsible for the Mahatma's life. Each one did what he could to save that precious life. Temples were thrown open to Untouchables, who had been barred from them for thousands of years. Village wells were shared with Untouchables, who had been forced to get their water from drainage ditches. High-caste Hindus dined publicly with Untouchable garbage collectors, and schools admitted the children of Untouchables. Roads and streets previously closed to Outcastes were opened to them at last.

Meanwhile, Hindu leaders met with the Untouchable leader, Dr. Ambedkar, and worked feverishly to come to an agreement.

Ambedkar gloried in his position of power. He knew that he had Gandhi's life in his hands. Only he could make a pact with the Hindus that would induce the Mahatma to break his fast. Remembering the oppression, the cruelty, and the degradation that his people had suffered for centuries, Ambedkar in revenge drove a hard bargain.

Gandhi was sinking fast. He lay on his white iron cot in the shade of a mango tree in the prison yard, listless and unmoving. During his previous fasts, he had remained relatively healthy and fairly strong. But during other fasts he had taken sensible precautions. He had always drunk water regularly, and he submitted to massage to relieve the aching of his wasting body. This time he was too anxious, too upset about the future of the Untouchables. He did not care what happened to him. He drank little water, and he refused massage.

On the third day of his fast, prison authorities, fearful that Gandhi was dying on their hands, sent for Kasturbai.

She walked toward her husband, shaking her head reprovingly. "Again, the same story," she scolded.

For the first time in days, Gandhi smiled.

"I will massage you," she announced, and he submitted meekly. After that, Kasturbai took entire charge of him.

On the following day, Friday, the doctors agreed that Gandhi's condition was critical. He might die at any minute. But he lasted out the day . . . and the night . . . and the next day.

By that time Hindu leaders had reached a compromise with Ambedkar. However, Gandhi refused to

During Gandhi's many prison terms, loyal Kasturbai often took his place as speaker and political leader.

break his fast until the agreement had been ratified by England's prime minister.

The text of the pact was wired to London. It was Sunday, and the prime minister was not in his office. An urgent message was sent to his country home.

At last the welcome news came to Yeravda prison where Gandhi lay: the Yeravda Pact had been approved. Gandhi could break his fast. A hymn was sung, then Gandhi accepted orange juice from Kasturbai.

All of India rejoiced.

Untouchability was not immediately removed by Gandhi's "epic fast," but never again would it meet with public approval. Untouchability was definitely doomed.

16.   A Martyr for Muslims

Soon after the "Epic Fast," Gandhi was released from jail. However, the rest of his life was a succession of prison terms—in total, he spent 2,338 days in jail. Kasturbai too was arrested time after time; in one two-year period, she was imprisoned six times.

Gandhi came to the conclusion that Congress followed his lead, not because the members believed in nonviolence and a return to the Simple Life, but because they loved and admired him personally. Jawaharlal Nehru in particular believed that India must progress in science and technology if she was ever to take her place with other modern nations.

Gandhi felt that he should not influence the Congress to act against the convictions of its members, so he withdrew from it.

He started a new paper to replace *Young India*, which had been suppressed by the government. Through its pages he tried to educate the people in matters of sanitation and nutrition.

Adoring throngs of people crowd about the Mahatma's rickshaw as he visits the British viceroy in 1940.

"Milk and bananas make a perfect meal," he wrote. "Green leaves added to the diet of villagers will enable them to avoid many diseases. Hand-pounded rice is far better for the health than machine-polished grain, which removes essential vitamins. Peanuts are very nutritious and relatively inexpensive." He gave detailed instructions for preparing each food.

Gandhi's correspondence was now huge. He received an average of 100 letters a day from all over the world. His secretary Mahadev sorted them and answered most of them, but Gandhi himself replied to a staggering number by hand. He loved to write postcards or to scribble an answer on the back of an old envelope. He always used the stub of an old pencil, never a new one. When his right hand grew tired, he used his left.

The Mahatma was besieged by a steady stream of callers. Mahadev supervised the visits and tried to limit the demands on the Mahatma's time and energy.

When World War II broke out in 1939, the government announced that India, as part of the British Empire, was now at war with Germany. None of India's leaders had been consulted, and the people were indignant. The government refused Nehru's plea to make definite promises of self-rule for India in return for assistance in the war. Indians who spoke out against the war were jailed; 23,000 were imprisoned in a single year. Feeling against the British rose higher and higher. Again the Congress turned to Gandhi for advice.

On August 8, 1942, the Indian National Congress, meeting in Bombay, passed a "Quit India" resolution.

"British rule in India must end immediately," Congress announced. "Unless this is done Congress will be reluctantly compelled to start a civil disobedience campaign, under the leadership of Mahatma Gandhi."

That evening Gandhi addressed the meeting. "Before we begin the campaign," he said, "I will plead with the viceroy to accept the Congress' demands. Then I will tell you my plans."

The viceroy did not wait for Gandhi to plead with him. Before dawn he placed the Mahatma, Nehru, and other Indian leaders under arrest and put them in jail. The main prison was already full, so Gandhi, his secretary Mahadev, and several others were taken to an improvised prison in the huge rambling palace of the Aga Khan near Yeravda.

The following day Kasturbai announced, "Since my husband has been arrested, I myself will deliver the speech he planned to give in Bombay." She was promptly arrested and taken to the Aga Khan's palace to join her husband.

The viceroy expected Gandhi's arrest to eliminate the threat of violence, but it worked exactly the opposite. So angry were the people that riots broke out. Government buildings were burned. British officials were assaulted. Telegraph lines were destroyed, railroads demolished, and roads obstructed.

The viceroy blamed Gandhi for all this destruction, but the Mahatma refused to accept the responsibility. He knew that if he had been left free, he could have controlled the mobs.

"It was the government," Gandhi wrote to the viceroy, "that goaded the people to the point of madness."

In protest against the viceroy's unfairness in blaming him, and the viceroy's refusal to cooperate with the Congress, the Mahatma undertook a 21-day fast. Still the viceroy would not apologize and made no move toward meeting the demands of Congress. So the fast dragged on for the full three weeks. Gandhi survived it better than he had the shorter fast against Untouchability, but the country resented the necessity for it. The viceroy's behavior plunged British-Indian relations to a new low.

During the first week of Gandhi's imprisonment, Mahadev, his devoted secretary and constant companion for 24 years, died of a heart attack. Now Gandhi turned more and more to Kasturbai. He wanted her with him all the time, and the prison officials permitted it; they were allowed considerable freedom within their prison.

During the two years that the aging couple were imprisoned in the Aga Khan's palace, Gandhi resumed his efforts to educate his wife. By now she had learned to read and write a little, but geography, history, and science were mysteries to her.

One day Gandhi was testing her on the geography he had been teaching her. "Lahore is the capital of one of India's eleven provinces," he said. "Which province is it?"

Kasturbai thought hard. "Calcutta?"

"Calcutta is a city," Gandhi reminded her, "not a province. Lahore is the capital of Bengal."

They laughed together. "Let's play a game instead

of studying," Kasturbai suggested. "Let's play *carrom*." This was her favorite game, a kind of shuffleboard. Gandhi joined her, smiling indulgently.

In December, 1943, Kasturbai fell ill. Prison doctors, Indian physicians, and nature-cure experts all did their best, but nothing proved effective.

For hours at a time the Mahatma sat by his wife's bed. He asked the prison authorities to send for their sons and grandsons. All came promptly except Harilal, the eldest, who had broken with his family some years back. A failure at business, he blamed his troubles on his father's lack of interest in him and began drinking heavily. At last Harilal too arrived, but he was so drunk he had to be removed from his mother's presence.

On February 22, 1944, Kasturbai lay with her head resting in her husband's lap. "I am going now," she told him faintly. "We have known many joys and sorrows together." Then she died.

Her death was a great blow to Gandhi. They had been married more than 62 years.

A few weeks later Gandhi himself, now 75, fell sick, and the government released him from jail. Although he did not know it, his last prison term had ended.

Until the Mahatma was out of prison and could talk freely again with other Indian leaders, he did not realize how the political situation in India had worsened.

For years tension between Hindus and Muslims had

been building; Gandhi's fast for Hindu-Muslim unity had helped only temporarily. Now there was bitter enmity between them, and the man most responsible for the hostility was the Muslim leader Jinnah.

Jinnah was Gandhi's opposite in nearly every way: tall instead of short; smartly dressed instead of half-naked; vain and ambitious instead of humble; haughty and stern in place of cheerful and fun-loving.

Jinnah wanted India split into two nations. He believed that the Muslims would not be treated fairly in a united country, because the Hindus outnumbered them three to one.

The idea of dividing India into two nations shocked the Mahatma. "I would as soon be cut in two myself!" he protested. "Hindus and Muslims are all Indians. Notwithstanding the differences between Hinduism and Islam, we all worship the same God. There is no reason why we can not live together in peace."

World War II ended on August 14, 1945. A year later England at last promised definitely to give India freedom. A so-called interim government was set up to rule the country until the new Indian government could take over. An English viceroy still headed the government, but Indians were appointed to the other posts.

For the first time, an Indian, Jawaharlal Nehru, became prime minister of India. Jinnah, the Muslim leader, was angry that the viceroy had not chosen him prime minister. He refused to accept any other office or cooperate with the interim government. Instead, he declared August 16, 1946 "Direct Action Day" for Muslims.

To the horror of all India, "Direct Action" turned out to be savage riots. Four days of bloody fighting in Calcutta resulted in 5,000 killed and 15,000 injured, mostly Hindus. It became known as the "Great Calcutta Killing." The violence soon spread. It became a religious civil war.

For the Mahatma there was nothing to be done but go to the scenes of the worst rioting and try to calm

Nehru, left, had become prime minister of India, but he presided over a strife-torn and bleeding nation.

the mobs. For months he traveled from village to village and from city to city. His very presence seemed to have a soothing effect. Wherever he went, he left peace and brotherhood behind him. But before his work was finished in one place, violence broke out in another.

Early in 1947 a new viceroy, Lord Louis Mountbatten, who would be the last, came to India. He would supervise the formation of an independent Indian government.

Lord Mountbatten began to arrange for an orderly transfer of power from the British to the Indians. He sent for the leaders of the Hindus and Muslims, Nehru and Jinnah, and he asked Gandhi to act as an adviser.

Agreement seemed impossible. Jinnah would settle for nothing less than a separate nation for Muslims.

Finally Mountbatten gave in. A separate country, Pakistan, was carved out of predominantly Muslim provinces at the northeast and northwest corners of India. The new country was in two parts, with the great mass of India in between. Worse, the provinces assigned to Pakistan contained millions of Hindus, and there were many Muslims left in India.

To the very last Gandhi opposed the plan of two nations, but other Indian leaders wanted independence at any price, and the partition plan was adopted.

On August 15, 1947, India became independent. Although Gandhi had worked for this day for 32 years, he could take no joy in it. India was free, yes. Indians would govern their land at last. But it was a torn, bleeding country, not the proud, free, united nation he had dreamed of.

Even after Pakistan was established, violence continued. Hindus tried to drive Muslims out of India and take their property, while Muslims in Pakistan did the same to the Hindus there.

For months Calcutta had been the scene of continual riots. In August, 1947, Gandhi went to the strife-torn city to try to calm stormy tempers. He thought he had succeeded when he saw Muslims and Hindus embracing each other in the streets and shouting "Long live Mahatma Gandhi!"

But the peace was only superficial. One night about 10 P.M. Gandhi was aroused by angry voices. Then he heard crashing glass, tramping feet, shouting voices, and pounding on his door. He got out of bed and opened the door to see a group of furious Muslims.

Gandhi placed his palms together under his chin in the Hindu greeting, and murmured a blessing. But the hoodlums were in no mood for religious gestures. One of them threw a brick at him, which missed by inches. Another struck at him with a pole.

The Mahatma stood silent. He was in obvious peril from the maddened Muslims, but he did not retreat an inch or betray any fear.

As the intruders made ready to attack him again, the police arrived and the mob soon dispersed.

Gandhi left Calcutta on September 7 for Delhi, where riots also raged. The capital was full of refugees. There were Hindu and Sikh refugees who had come from Pakistan, and Muslims who were trying to escape from India into Pakistan. Nearly 15,000,000 people were fleeing from one land to the other. Fighting between the two religious groups was almost constant.

There was no room for the Mahatma in the Untouchables' quarter where he usually stayed when he went to Delhi, so he stayed in the home of his long-time friend, the millionaire G. D. Birla. Gandhi insisted on having the fine furniture taken out of his room. He wanted to live simply, according to his custom, with only his spinning wheel, a cot, and a mat to sit on.

Day after day the Mahatma visited refugee camps, bringing all the food and blankets he could collect in the city. The hunger, sickness, and unhappiness he saw made his heart ache. Several times a day he spoke to crowds of bitter, impoverished refugees. In spite of the danger in Delhi, he refused to have an armed guard.

Each evening Gandhi held a prayer meeting on the spacious terraces of Birla House. Each evening he would ask, "Does anyone object to the reading of some verses from the *Koran*?"

Usually a few of the Hindus present objected.

"Would you remain quiet during the reading?" he asked.

Always the objectors agreed, and verses from the *Koran* were read, as well as portions of the *Gita*. As the days passed, the people of Delhi learned that they did not have to agree in order to live side by side without violence. It was only necessary to respect others.

Delhi became quieter, but violence still flared occasionally in and around the city.

Once more Gandhi fell back on the technique that had never failed to bring peace—he undertook a fast unto death. "I will break my fast when there is genuine peace between Muslims and Hindus," he said.

From the moment the fast began, Nehru and other leaders of the new Indian nation tried to bring the warring factions together. The Indian government gave to the Pakistan government a large sum of money that had been owed since partition. A pledge of peace and brotherhood was signed by a hundred prominent men. They all went to Birla House to tell Gandhi. He was assured that Muslims who had fled from the city could now return safely and conduct their business as before.

The Mahatma remained silent for a long time, thinking. Everyone present watched tensely, scarcely daring to breathe. Finally he spoke.

"I will break my fast."

That evening the Mahatma held his usual prayer

meeting out on the terrace. Hundreds of people attended it. Gandhi had to be carried out in a chair, because he was too weak to walk. He told the crowd about the pledge, and he said, "I interpret this pledge to mean that come what may, there will be complete friendship between Hindus, Muslims, Christians, and Jews, a friendship not to be broken." This had been Gandhi's dream as long as he could remember.

On January 30, 1948, Gandhi, now 78, left his room in Birla House for the terrace to attend his prayer meeting. As usual, he walked between two devoted young women, leaning his forearms on their shoulders.

About 500 people had gathered for the meeting. As Gandhi and the girls approached the crowd, the people rose to greet their Mahatma. Many fell to the ground before him. Gandhi made the gesture of greeting and blessed them.

Then a young Hindu edged forward through the closely pressed throng. He bent low as if he intended to fall at the Mahatma's feet. Instead, he whipped out a pistol and fired three shots in quick succession.

"Oh, God!" Gandhi gasped and collapsed.

From all sides came screams, shouts, and sobs. Somebody grabbed the assassin and held him until the police arrived. Somebody else went for a doctor, but it was useless; the Mahatma had died instantly. Loving hands lifted his body and carried it into the house.

His sons and close friends were sent for. Nehru, prime minister of India, came at once. Gandhi's death was a terrible blow for him. He had loved the Mahatma all of his adult life. Although he had disagreed with him about politics, he had never failed to admire and revere him.

It was Nehru's sad duty to break the news to the nation by radio:

> The light has gone out of our lives. . . .
> Our beloved leader, Bapu, as we call him,
> the father of our nation, is no more. . . .

The light has gone out, I said, and yet I was wrong . . . a thousand years later that light will still be seen in this country, and the world will see it and it will give solace to innumerable hearts. For that light represented the living truth . . . the eternal man was with us with his eternal truth, reminding us of the right path, drawing us from error, taking this ancient country to freedom. . . .

Pakistanis realized that Gandhi had really been martyred for them, because he defended their rights. Even those who had hated him understood now that he had been their best friend. The two countries, India and Pakistan, began to learn to live side by side peaceably.

It is doubtful that any man was ever mourned by as many people as Mahatma Gandhi.

A few years before Gandhi's death, India's great poet Rabindranath Tagore wrote about him prophetically:

Perhaps he will not succeed. Perhaps he will fail as the Buddha failed and as Christ failed to wean men from their iniquities, but he will always be remembered as one who made his life a lesson for all ages to come.

Glossary

ahimsa: ancient Hindu teaching of nonviolence

ashram: religious community. Men noted for their holiness and learning live there.

ba: Indian word for mother

bapu: Indian word for father

behn: kindly way of addressing a woman. It also means sister.

Bhagavad Gita: sacred poem of 700 stanzas called the *Song of God*

Brahman: the first of the four Hindu castes. Its members are priests and scholars.

Chaturmas: a four-month season of rain in India. Vows to fast are made during this period.

darshan: a spiritual blessing; spiritual happiness that comes from being close to a cherished person, place, or thing

dharma: religious duty, moral law

hartal: work stoppage; time of prayer and fasting

kansar: wedding sweet made of wheat and traditionally served to the wedded couple after the ceremony

khadi: a hand-spun or home-spun cloth

Kshatriya: second Hindu caste whose members were rulers and warriors

saptapadi: seven steps a Hindu bride and bridegroom must take together while making promises of mutual devotion

sari: a garment of long cloth worn by Hindu women

satyagraha: force born of love and truth

satyagrahis: those who practice satyagraha

sheth: master. This is a name given to Hindus of importance.

Shudra: the fourth Hindu caste whose members are laborers and peasants

Vaisya: the third Hindu caste whose members are farmers and merchants

Chronological List of Events
in Gandhi's Life

1869   On October 2, Mohandas K. Gandhi is born in Porbandar, western India, to parents of the merchant, or Vaisya, caste.

1882   In accordance with Hindu custom, Mohandas is married at age 13 to Kasturbai Nakanji, the daughter of a Porbandar merchant.

1888   Gandhi leaves his family in India to study law in England.

1891   After passing his bar examinations, Gandhi returns to India as a lawyer.

1893   At the age of 24, Gandhi goes to South Africa to handle a law case for a Porbandar business concern. Shocked by the discrimination practiced against Indians living in South Africa, he begins working in their behalf.

1899   War breaks out in South Africa between the British and the Dutch, or Boers, both of whom want to control the area.

1901   The war ends, and the British now rule all of South Africa.

1908   Gandhi gives up his law practice and dedicates his life to leading the Indian people in their struggle for social and political equality.

1910   Gandhi starts Tolstoy Farm, near Johannesburg, where Indians work and live together.

1913 Gandhi organizes marches to resist South African laws which were unfair to Indians.

1914 Gandhi and his family return to India, where he organizes an *ashram,* or religious retreat.

1918 World War I ends on November 11, but India is not given self-government by Britain. Instead, she is oppressed more than ever by the despised Rowlatt Bills.

1920 Gandhi drafts a new constitution for the Indian National Congress and soon becomes the dominant political figure in India. He is now called the Mahatma (Great Soul). Gandhi stresses a campaign of noncooperation with the British.

1922 Gandhi is arrested for printing articles in his newspaper against British rule. At his trial, which becomes known as "The Great Trial," Gandhi is sentenced to six years in jail.

1924 Following an attack of appendicitis, Gandhi is released from prison after serving only two years of his sentence.

1928 The Indian National Congress asks the government of England for dominion status, or self-rule within the Empire, by the end of the year.

1929 The Congress instructs Gandhi to lead a campaign against Britain. He does so by conducting a salt march, in which thousands walk to the seashore and, in defiance of British law, make their own salt. Gandhi is imprisoned.

1931   Gandhi attends the Second Round Table Conference in London.

1932   Gandhi protests a new British law which would permanently separate the Hindus, Muslims, and Untouchables into separate political groups. He fasts for seven days in an "Epic Fast" until a compromise, the Yeravda Pact, is reached.

1942   The Indian National Congress passes a "Quit India" resolution, stating that British rule must end immediately. As head of the campaign, Gandhi is arrested and jailed in Yeravda prison.

1944   Gandhi's wife, Kasturbai, dies on February 22, after 62 years of marriage. On May 6, Gandhi is released from jail for the final time.

1946   Britain promises freedom to India, but Jinnah, the Muslim leader, insists on a separate nation. Rioting breaks out between Hindus and Muslims.

1947   India and Pakistan, as separate nations, become independent of Britain on August 15.

1948   On January 30, at the age of 78, Gandhi is assassinated on his way to a prayer meeting.

Index